Fooling with Words

Fooling with Words

A CELEBRATION OF POETS
AND THEIR CRAFT

Bill Moyers

WILLIAM MORROW AND COMPANY, INC.

New York

Permissions, constituting a continuation of the copyright page,
appear on pages 226–230.

It is the policy of William Morrow and Company, Inc., and its imprints
and affiliates, recognizing the importance of preserving what has been
written, to print the books we publish on acid-free paper, and we exert
our best efforts to that end.

Library of Congress Cataloging-in-Publication Data

Fooling with words : a celebration of poets and their craft /
Bill Moyers.—1st ed.
p.   cm.
ISBN 0-688-17346-2
1. Poetics.   2. Poetry—Authorship.   I. Moyers, Bill D.
PN1042.F58   1999
808.1—dc21   99–34965
CIP

Printed in the United States of America

First Edition

1   2   3   4   5   6   7   8   9   10

BOOK DESIGN BY JO ANNE METSCH

www.williammorrow.com

ACKNOWLEDGMENTS

"PRAISE THE BRIDGE that carried you over," advises a character in *The Heir-at-Law*. So I wish to thank the many people whose collaboration brought this book to safe passage. Scott McVay and the trustees of the Geraldine R. Dodge Foundation head the list, because without them there would have been no Dodge Poetry Festival, and without the festival there would be no book. Scott has now retired as executive director of the foundation, but if the poetry world could afford twenty-one-gun salutes for its heroes, there would have been no end of deafening praise in his honor when he stepped down after twenty-three years. Fortunately, Scott's colleague James Haba remains as festival director. Jim composes the festival every two years as if it were a poem. That will surprise no one who knows him as a poet in his own right. His poem "Yes to Blue" goes to the heart of the creative process and the spirit of the Dodge Poetry Festival:

Yes to Blue

Yes to blue after trying
to separate green from yellow
and hoping that everything
will get simpler each time
you bring an idea closer
to the light which is always
changing always being
born
day after day
year after year
again and again
now

Catherine Tatge and Dominique Lasseur produced and directed our coverage of the 1998 Dodge Poetry Festival for public television, ably assisted by Joel Katz, Joel Shapiro, Dahvi Waller, and Sarah Duxbury. Judith Davidson Moyers and Judy Doctoroff O'Neill were executive producers of the special, and Judith collaborated closely with me in shaping this book while Judy cast a careful eye on the manuscript at critical times. My executive assistant, Friema Norkin, has lent her enthusiasm and hard work to this project from its inception. Debbie Rubenstein, whose good humor survived unforgiving deadlines, a weekly melee of details, and my open warfare with the computer, managed the publication process. She is our indispensable ringmaster. I also am indebted to Betty Sue Flowers, my friend and collaborator at the University of Texas, for encouraging me to do this book and for urging me to let the poets speak in their own voices.

The two-hour documentary and ten half-hour programs featuring individual poets were made possible, as we say on PBS, by Mutual of America Life Insurance Company, the John D. and Catherine T. MacArthur Foundation, and the Herb Alpert Foundation. Herb's trumpet sent my soul soaring the first time I heard him thirty-five years ago. He, his wife, Lani Hall, and Kip Cohen are kindred spirits.

I have been delighted by the experience of working for the first time with Meaghan Dowling, senior editor at William Morrow and Company, whose judgment and deft skills rescued me from one cul-de-sac after another. And how could I not be grateful to my old friend Marly Rusoff, Morrow's associate publisher and director of marketing, who responded so quickly and positively when I called to suggest this book? Thanks go to Phillip

Falcone for adapting swiftly and graciously to our ever-changing permissions needs.

Above all, I wish to thank the poets who generously cooperated with us in the preparation of this book: Coleman Barks, Lorna Dee Cervantes, Mark Doty, Deborah Garrison, Jane Hirshfield, Stanley Kunitz, Kurtis Lamkin, Shirley Geok-lin Lim, Paul Muldoon, Marge Piercy, and Robert Pinsky. I relished their company at the festival as I reveled in their words.

CONTENTS

INTRODUCTION

THIS BOOK IS about some poets I know.

It's not about the technical properties of their work. While any serious student of poetry will want to understand assonance, syntax, dimeters, and couplets—and has no shortage of informed sources to consult—this is not a book for the experts. I am a journalist, not a literary critic; the only sure thing I can tell you about poetry is that I like it. The sounds of poems are pleasing to me, and I enjoy a poem read aloud even when I do not wholly understand it. Talking to poets about their lives also makes their poetry more accessible to me. Once I know how a poet feels about a granddaughter or a father's death or about hiding under the steps to read while other kids were playing soccer, I am more likely to hear the poet's voice in the poem. Just as I read biographies of political leaders to see their lives in context, so I like to know about the experiences that produced the poet. Perhaps this desire to see the human side of the art is the reason I am a journalist instead of a critic.

For most people, poetry is a solitary affair, like meditation or prayer. Edward Hirsch, in his fine new book on how to read a poem, describes poetry as "a passionately private communication from a soul to another soul" and the best time for reading as "the middle of the night." Robert Frost urged readers "to settle down like a revolving door and make ourselves at home among the poems, completely at our ease as to how they should be taken." I do this myself at odd times both night and day, randomly picking up one of the poetry books scattered around the house and allowing its poems to address me as they will, like letters from old friends. The seductions and demands of modern life, however, compete for the quiet time needed for poems, and occasionally it is reported that poetry's reading constituency is eroding. One recent essay lamented the failure of any contemporary poet to achieve the superstar status of a Robert Frost, Edna St. Vincent Millay, or Wallace Stevens. If that is so, it may be, as Martin Arnold has written in *The New York Times*, because "there is no one American language" in which poetry can speak as it did in a more homogeneous culture. This "nation of nations" contains more nations than ever, with more poems being written, more readers to read them, more voices to speak them, and more ears to hear them.

The result is a resurgence of poetry on the public stage, a phenomenon that caught my journalist's curiosity early in the nineties. David Lehman writes, in the Foreword to *The Best American Poetry 1998*, that "the nation's hot romance with poetry shows no sign of cooling off." The prestige of the art form, he says, has steadily climbed since this decade began. As evidence he offers the proliferating poetry websites, the public response to Poet Laureate Robert Pinsky's Favorite Poem project (see p. 213), Andrew Carroll's cross-country odyssey to distribute poetry books to hotels for placement alongside the Gideon Bible, the inclusion of poetry books as "standard features" in all new Volkswagen cars during National Poetry Month, and the celebration of poetry at events from the White House gathering of poets hosted by the Clintons to poetry slams in smoky downtown bars. In the spring of 1999, just blocks from my office on the West Side of New York, an estimated five thousand people turned out for the People's Poetry Festival sponsored by Poets House and City Lore, including seven hundred hardy souls who showed up for a reading of Edgar Allan Poe's poems in an East Village cemetery at midnight on a chilly Saturday night.

Poetry is not only a private act between consenting

poet and reader, it is a public act as well. I have seen poems work their magic on thousands of people at once. The effect can be physical, like the "breathless arousal" that attended religious revivals in my native South. The effect can be sensual; Stanley Kunitz writes, "Every new poem is like finding a new bride. Words are so erotic, they never tire of their coupling." The effect can be intellectual, quietly opening the mind to a new way of seeing—as Mary Oliver's white owl becomes "a buddha with wings." And it can be spiritual, a moment of transcendence, like the mystery of communion in a congregation of believers.

I do not understand the power of poetry to transfigure, but I remember the first time I experienced it. We had been studying composition in high school English, plowing through such necessary but rocky furrows as infinitives, genitives, and gerunds; the days were creaking by like turns of the torturer's rack. Then one morning Mrs. Hughes announced that we were changing course. We were going to study poetry. That is, she would read poems to us and we would listen, without commentary from her or questions from us. Inez Hughes could dissect a poem at ten paces with her eyes closed if she wished, but she insisted that poetry requires attention before it welcomes analysis.

So she read. Standing with her shoulders high and her back straight, and holding *The Oxford Book of English Verse* as far from her body as her arms would extend, she read. For the entire hour she read, until the bell rang and the spell was broken. She had a sonorous southern voice, as versatile as a pipe organ, which rose half an octave as she read. Between her native drawl and an exactness of diction acquired in elocution courses back east, her sentences could flow like a languid stream or break, crisp and distinct, like twigs snapping underfoot. She liked Blake:

From *Reeds of Innocence*

Piping down the valleys wild,
  Piping songs of pleasant glee,
On a cloud I saw a child,
  And he laughing said to me:

'Pipe a song about a Lamb!'
  So I piped with merry cheer.
'Piper, pipe that song again;'
  So I piped: he wept to hear.

She agreed with Wordsworth:

From *The World*

The world is too much with us; late and soon,
  Getting and spending, we lay waste our powers:
  Little we see in Nature that is ours. . . .

And she was haunted by Thomas Gray:

From *Elegy Written in a Country Churchyard*

The Curfew tolls the knell of parting day,
    The lowing herd wind slowly o'er the lea,
The plowman homeward plods his weary way,
    And leaves the world to darkness and to me.

She often read Gray's elegy, and as she did the poem took hold of me. Perhaps it was the rhythmic cadence: "The boast of heraldry, the pomp of pow'r." Or the romantic imagery: "Full many a flower is born to blush unseen." Or the stark reality: "The paths of glory lead but to the grave." Most certainly my teacher's voice left as much of an imprint on me as the poet's verse. Several years later, during my first visit to England, I heard her voice in my head the moment I spied the gravestones in the churchyard at Stoke Poges that Gray immortalized. Reaching the vista that seemed so unchanged from the poem's evocation of it, I shivered slightly. I felt as if I had been there before and was even now experiencing the setting and the emotion as Gray experienced them two centuries earlier. Only twenty-two at the time, I felt sadness at the transience of my own life and gratitude for the timelessness of all life. Thomas Gray may have felt nothing of the sort, of course; it may just have been the voice in my head, but such is poetry's power that the emotions awakened then are just as real to me now.

I was hooked that day in class, and Mrs. Hughes knew it. She began inviting me to her home, where she would read poems aloud as I devoured the cookies that she offered me. Occasionally she would hand me the book and suggest I read. But my adolescent voice sounded more like a rusty accordion than a pipe organ, and, after one or two poems, she would gracefully retrieve the book, pass more cookies, and read on, until the light drained from the window, only crumbs were left on the plate, and it was time to go. We continued these sessions practically every week through the winter.

Fortunately, Inez Hughes was one of four consecutive teachers—from my final two years in high school through the first two years in college—who believed in reading aloud to their students. Either widows or spinsters, they were married to the English language. Selma Brotze loved Shelley, Keats, and Byron (although, being a good Presbyterian, she never divulged if she knew about the latter's raging promiscuity; for her, the poet was a cracked vessel, the poem its delicious and unspoiled nectar, and it was important not to confuse the two). Mary Tom Osborne preferred Thackeray, Tennyson, and Shakespeare. Eva Joy McGuffin plumbed

Chaucer, Milton, and the Brownings, especially the Brownings. Widowed as a young mother with twins, she could barely hide her melancholy as she recited this by Elizabeth Barrett Browning:

Grief

I tell you, hopeless grief is passionless;
That only men incredulous of despair,
Half-taught in anguish, through the midnight air
Beat upward to God's throne in loud access
Of shrieking and reproach. Full desertness,
In souls as countries, lieth silent-bare
Under the blanching, vertical eye-glare
Of the absolute Heavens. Deep-hearted man, express
Grief for thy Dead in silence like to death—
Most like a monumental statute set
In everlasting watch and moveless woe
Till itself crumble to the dust beneath.
Touch it; the marble eyelids are not wet:
If it could weep, it could arise and go.

My own preferences were unaffected by critical analysis. I could not read the notes, but I loved the music. And that was just fine. While these teachers said that we would appreciate poems much more if we understood the virtues of iambic pentameter, allusion, and the resonance of repetition, they would not have us dismember a poem's anatomy at the risk of its soul, or squeeze meaning from it at the expense of delight. Looking back, I realize they simply believed in the magic of poetry's music and sought to expose us—even the tone-deaf among us—to the pleasure of listening to "the best words in the best order."

This early exposure to the sounds of poetry served me well when I turned to reading poems alone, especially a poem whose meaning was not readily apparent. Often, when I am reading silently, my mind will, on its own, apply the brakes in midsentence to spin down a side road to inquire into the author's purpose or point. The sure way back, I find, is to follow the advice offered by Robert Pinsky later in this book: "Read [the poem] aloud. And don't worry about interpreting it, or emulating Gielgud." Pinsky says that poetry is a vocal art that requires a physical response. "If you fall in love with a person, a cuisine, an animal, or a sport, in time you'll want to analyze it, know the history of it, and know what intelligent people think about it. But the first thing is—you like to pet the animal, eat the food, look at the person." Just so with a poem: "Read it aloud to relish the consonants and vowels and the way the verbs and adjectives and nouns do their job." Once you hear the music, you can probe for meaning or for the sources of creativity and craft. In his own book Edward Hirsch writes: "Poems communicate before they are understood. . . . Let the poem work in you as a human experience. Listen to the words, and pay attention to the feelings they evoke."

I must report that my youthful exhilaration at the music of poetry did not make a poet of me, a loss the world has somehow not bothered to grieve. I did write one poem in high school that was entered, without my knowledge, in a schoolwide competition. When it won third place I was unexpectedly called upon to read it during the awards assembly, provoking a spasm of guffaws among a row of burly athletes. They proved to be discerning critics. Shortly before her death a few years ago, Selma Brotze discovered a faded copy of that poem in a box in her attic. She sent it to me with a note written with her usual affection and candor: "I enjoyed reading it again, but you made the correct choice in giving up poetry for journalism."

The world was spared a mediocre poet, but poetry could not escape my journalistic ardor. Perhaps in remembrance of those teachers, perhaps just to indulge my own appetite for the sound of words, I have taken every opportunity to introduce an audience to contemporary poets through the medium of television. My favorite stop on the beat is the Geraldine R. Dodge Poetry Festival in the little restored village of Waterloo,

New Jersey, which every two years is transformed into "Poetry Heaven." More than three hundred established and emerging poets have taken part in the Dodge Festival since it was first held in 1986, and more than fifty thousand people have come to hear their poems. I cannot recall seeing anywhere else so many happy people in one place. At a political convention the revelry is often forced—merrymaking fomented as propaganda. The opening roars of a sporting event soon dissolve into disappointment for half of the players and onlookers, who will go home muttering about bums, umpires, coaches, or score. At the poetry festival the joy lasts, poets are cheered, and everyone wins.

The festival invites conversation with poets, and the interviews in this book were conducted there in the fall of 1998. I listened to poets read to large crowds in the main tent and to small workshops scattered around the village. Then I asked them to talk with me about a few of their poems, some of the life experiences that had shaped their work, and the public appeal of poetry today. It was during just such a discussion that Coleman Barks gave me the title for this book. Waving an arm toward strollers reading from poetry books, couples reading to each other behind curtains of obliviousness, and young people dancing to poetry under the cupolas, Coleman looked as if he had fallen into a garden of everlasting bliss, as he exclaimed: "It's amazing that so many people can be genuinely excited about fooling with words."

Fooling with words is the play of poets. They alone understand how much hard work it is. But none I know would have it otherwise, for poems are born this way.

Fooling with Words

STANLEY KUNITZ

*T*HE APPLAUSE BEGINS *as Stanley Kunitz rises from the front row, makes his way up the steps, and strides across the stage toward the lectern, his arms swinging gaily at his sides. In his right hand he carries a collection of poems, which he places on the small podium while reaching with his other hand for the inside pocket of his lime green coat, fishing for his glasses. The applause has turned to cheers. He is a familiar and revered figure here. Now people are on their feet. Their* hurrahs *ricochet around the tent, and the noise of four thousand clapping hands sounds like rain on the canvas roof. Kunitz stands motionless at the microphone, his slight figure no more imposing than a sparrow. He is a shy man, and modest, and he isn't sure how to respond. Then a small smile creases his white mustache, he lifts a hand to*

· I ·

acknowledge the reception, and opens the book of poems. Once again, the applause soars before the audience settles back to listen.

Out beyond the tent America is trapped in a media warp of Monicamania, where words are tipped in toxin and hurled like red-hot missiles in a rhetorical nuclear war. Here, inside this hushed sanctuary, Stanley Kunitz, acknowledging "the dark news emanating from the capital," reads a poem he had been moved to write during "the even darker days of Watergate." The poem—"The Lincoln Relics"—recalls an exhibit he once saw in Washington of the contents found in the pocket of the sixteenth president on the night of his assassination. The "watchfob and ivory pocket knife, / a handkerchief of Irish linen, / a button severed from his sleeve," a five-dollar Confederate note, and the gold-rimmed spectacles "mended with a loop of string" made, for the poet, "a noble, dissolving music out of homely fife and drum." Addressing the slain president, whose innocence "was to trust / the better angels of our nature, / even when the Union cracked / and furious blood / ran north and south / along the lines of pillage," Kunitz asks, "in this Imperial City, / awash in gossip and power, / . . . Has no one told you / how the slow blood leaks / from your secret wound?"

There is not a sound in the tent, except for the quiet intensity of the poet's voice. He tells of taking a night walk along the Potomac, "searching for the prairie star, / westward scanning the horizon / for its eloquent and magnanimous light, /

yearning to be touched by its fire:" The longing in the poem is palpable in the tent, and as this very young old man, age ninety-three, descends from the stage, the audience stands in a tumult of applause. In a rational world, I tell myself, Stanley Kunitz would be Time *magazine's Man of the Century—not for armies commanded, cures discovered, or nations saved but because, through a discordant century of furious change, his voice—the poet's voice—speaks to what Lincoln himself called "the mystic chords of memory."*

Let's begin with a remembrance of long ago.

I was five years old when Halley's Comet visited Worcester, Massachusetts, the city of my birth, in 1910. When I was near ninety, the memory of that encounter, which had been simmering so long, finally emerged in the shape of a poem.

Halley's Comet

Miss Murphy in first grade
wrote its name in chalk
across the board and told us
it was roaring down the stormtracks
of the Milky Way at frightful speed
and if it wandered off its course

and smashed into the earth
there'd be no school tomorrow.
A red-bearded preacher from the hills
with a wild look in his eyes
stood in the public square
at the playground's edge
proclaiming he was sent by God
to save every one of us,
even the little children.
"Repent, ye sinners!" he shouted,
waving his hand-lettered sign.
At supper I felt sad to think
that it was probably
the last meal I'd share
with my mother and my sisters;
but I felt excited too
and scarcely touched my plate.
So mother scolded me
and sent me early to my room.
The whole family's asleep
except for me. They never heard me steal
into the stairwell hall and climb
the ladder to the fresh night air.

Look for me, Father, on the roof
of the red brick building
at the foot of Green Street—

that's where we live, you know, on the top floor.
I'm the boy in the white flannel gown
sprawled on this coarse gravel bed
searching the starry sky,
waiting for the world to end.

You saw Halley's Comet in 1910. You've lived under every president from Teddy Roosevelt to Bill Clinton—seventeen in all. You've lived through the First World War, the Great Depression, the Second World War (in which you served), Vietnam, the Teapot Dome scandal and Watergate, the arrival of the automobile and the plane, moving pictures, radio and television, and computers and the Internet; you watched the landing on the moon and wrote about it—

So much history!—and all of it interwoven with one's own story, the legend of a life. Poetry, I have argued, is ultimately mythology, the telling of the soul's passage through the valley of this life, its adventure in time, in history.

In your poem "The Layers" you say, "I have walked through many lives, / some of them my own, / and I am not who I was, / though some principle of being / abides, from which I struggle / not to stray." What is the essential Kunitz that still abides?

Isn't that for others to say? The answer, in any case, is implicit in the poems. But I must tell you that your query takes me all the way back to a troubled year at school when I stumbled on a sentence in one of Keats's letters that struck me with the force of revelation: "I am certain of nothing but the holiness of the Heart's affections and the truth of Imagination." Those are words that helped me on my way. And they still walk with me.

What is it that makes the heart's affections holy?

In a world without friendship and love, how could we even begin to understand the meaning of the sacred?

What do you love most?

Most of all, I love being alive. I love the natural world—and caring and creative people—and the seekers of justice and truth. Whom do I disdain? Bigots, reactionaries, self-righteous people, zealots, trimmers, bullies, and manipulators.

Your poem "The Long Boat" comes to a close with the lines "he loved the earth so much / he wanted to stay forever." Does that express your own feeling?

Of course!

Well, one reviewer recently referred to you as "Stanley Kunitz, poet of the twentieth century." If you keep on going, you're going to be poet of the twenty-first century!

I never expected to survive into the next millennium, but now I'm really gunning for it.

What do you have to say for growing old?

I won't deny that the flesh grows weary. But what continues to surprise me is that the unrelenting awareness that time is running out has only served to intensify my zest for art and life. As for that special and inimitable taste of self, that Gerard Manley Hopkins defined as being more distinctive than the taste of ale or alum or the smell of walnut leaf or camphor, the only significant change I can detect is that it has grown more bittersweet with the years. Inevitably age brings us closer to our ancestors. We begin to understand that each of us in turn is a bearer of news from the gene pool. I like to think that the poetic imagination is tuned in to that very source. Our memories run deeper than we know.

When you look back on the body of your work—all the poems you've written through the years—do you have favorites?

As you might expect, since poetry is such an intimate art, poets tend to favor their more recent productions. A poet in his age who chooses to read his early love poems in public must be prepared to risk appearing somewhat out of focus. A couple of my later poems come to mind that I especially enjoy sharing with others, in that they have such palpable connection with my present state of being. Would you like to hear them?

Certainly.

Here is a poem that owes its existence to decades of labor in my seaside garden on the Cape, the garden I created out of a barren sandhill—my "little Eden," as a poet-friend of mine has described it.

The Round

Light splashed this morning
on the shell-pink anemones
swaying on their tall stems;
down blue-spiked veronica
light flowed in rivulets
over the humps of the honeybees;
this morning I saw light kiss
the silk of the roses

in their second flowering,
my late bloomers
flushed with their brandy.
A curious gladness shook me.

So I have shut the doors of my house,
so I have trudged downstairs to my cell,
so I am sitting in semi-dark
hunched over my desk
with nothing for a view
to tempt me
but a bloated compost heap,
steamy old stinkpile,
under my window;
and I pick my notebook up
and I start to read aloud
the still-wet words I scribbled
on the blotted page:
"Light splashed . . ."

I can scarcely wait till tomorrow
when a new life begins for me,
as it does each day,
as it does each day.

Hearing you read that poem reminds me that renewal is one of your key themes.

Indeed it is. It has been one of my signature themes from the beginning. My very first collection—*Intellectual Things*, 1930—concluded with a poem I called "Vita Nuova" in acknowledgment of my debt to Dante. When I wrote it, I was in my early twenties, and the new life I envisioned then was a life in poetry.

Tell me about that other favorite poem of yours. Does it, too, deal with your theme of renewal?

How did you guess? I have a vivid memory of its origin only a few years ago in the midst of a furious late August storm on the Cape that told me we were nearing the end of summer, always a crucial time for me in the cycle of the year. The first line that came to me drifted in, as sometimes happens, from a poem I had written some forty years before; and the new lines flowed from it, as if they were a gift from the past, from another life.

Touch Me

Summer is late, my heart.
Words plucked out of the air
some forty years ago
when I was wild with love
and torn almost in two

scatter like leaves this night
of whistling wind and rain.
It is my heart that's late,
it is my song that's flown.
Outdoors all afternoon
under a gunmetal sky
staking my garden down,
I kneeled to the crickets trilling
underfoot as if about
to burst from their crusty shells;
and like a child again
marveled to hear so clear
and brave a music pour
from such a small machine.
What makes the engine go?
Desire, desire, desire.
The longing for the dance
stirs in the buried life.
One season only,

                and it's done.
So let the battered old willow
thrash against the windowpanes
and the house timbers creak.
Darling, do you remember
the man you married? Touch me,
remind me who I am.

After you read that poem to the audience here, there were cheers, whistles, applause, shouts of "Bravo! Bravo!" It was a remarkable response.

People who come to hear poetry are very generous. There's a curious relationship between the poet and his audience. Paul Celan, the great poet of the Holocaust, wrote cryptically that "a poem is solitary and on its way." In my interpretation, the poem is on its way in search of people. For its complete fulfillment it has to find an audience, it has to be invited into some other person's mind and heart. Once the poet lets go of his poem, it is no longer his. It belongs to anyone who wants it. It's a gift.

What has induced you to spend so much of your time and energy over the years in mentoring young poets and fostering their work?

The loneliness of my early years, when I desperately needed encouragement and companionship, ultimately led to a prolonged search for community. That need really directed my journey—the places I chose to live in, the friends I made, the poets' and artists' enclaves I visited or helped to found. And that is what brings me here now, as it has several times before, to the Geraldine R. Dodge Poetry Festival. Walt Whitman told us that

America is a nation of nations. The Dodge Festival demonstrates its faith in the spirit of American democracy by bringing together the many nations of our poetry.

Let's finish with a reading of "The Layers," from which we have already quoted. I have heard you describe it as a summing-up poem. What else can you say about it that would help us fill in the background?

I wrote it in the late seventies to conclude a collection of sixty years of my poetry. That was the turbulent decade of Watergate and Vietnam. Through the years I had endured the loss of several of my dearest friends, including Theodore Roethke, Mark Rothko, and—most recently—Robert Lowell. I felt I was near the end of a phase in my life and in my work. The poem began with two lines that came to me in a dream, spoken out of a dark cloud: "Live in the layers, / not on the litter."

The Layers

> I have walked through many lives,
> some of them my own,
> and I am not who I was,
> though some principle of being
> abides, from which I struggle

not to stray.
When I look behind,
as I am compelled to look
before I can gather strength
to proceed on my journey,
I see the milestones dwindling
toward the horizon
and the slow fires trailing
from the abandoned camp-sites,
over which scavenger angels
wheel on heavy wings.
Oh, I have made myself a tribe
out of my true affections,
and my tribe is scattered!
How shall the heart be reconciled
to its feast of losses?
In a rising wind
the manic dust of my friends,
those who fell along the way,
bitterly stings my face.
Yet I turn, I turn,
exulting somewhat,
with my will intact to go
wherever I need to go,
and every stone on the road
precious to me.
In my darkest night,

when the moon was covered
and I roamed through wreckage,
a nimbus-clouded voice
directed me:
"Live in the layers,
not on the litter."
Though I lack the art
to decipher it,
no doubt the next chapter
in my book of transformations
is already written.
I am not done with my changes.

Thank you, Stanley. Let's get together in the next millennium.

That's a date.

COLEMAN BARKS

*W*E SAT AMONG *the gravestones at the old cemetery just across the commons from the festival tent, talking about grandchildren. Not just any grandchildren, mind you. We were debating whose grandchildren are the most beautiful in the world—his or mine. Ballot after ballot produced one more tie vote, and we were stumped over how to break the impasse. Coleman Barks is a gentle fellow, with a voice like southern honey; the tousled hair falling across his temple and a graying beard beneath his dark deep-set eyes give him the aura of an ancient magnolia tree offering shelter and rest. But I have to tell you that on this matter of his granddaughter he is a stone wall, not to be moved. I assured him that being grandfather to the world's second most beautiful little girl is nothing to be ashamed of, but he would have none of it. Whipping out a pic-*

ture of her and thrusting it straight at the television camera, he demanded: "Let the world be the judge! Let the world vote and we'll see who comes in second!" I had never seen him so aroused. Ecstatic, yes; he is, after all, the best-known inter- preter today of the thirteenth-century Persian mystic poet Jelaluddin Rumi, whom Barks has helped make as popular in America as some pop stars. But Rumi's is the quiet ecstasy of the lover's sigh, and Barks is his calm accomplice. Since he would soon be performing with other poets in the great tent across the way, I decided to make a peace offering and end the competition that had so agitated him (he had no hope of win- ning anyway, as I had the last edit if not the last word). "Read me some of the poems you've written about her," I said. Imme- diately he grew calm, chuckling as he pulled a batch of pages from his packet. His granddaughter was given her great- grandmother's maiden name, Bryan. But Barks calls her Briny—as in the briny deep of the sea, where wonders reign.

Have you written many poems about Briny?

Oh, yes. I decided to do some shamelessly grandfa- therly poems this year. This first one is about the time I took her to the circus. One of those circuses over in Marietta, Georgia, where the performers turn out to be aging and inept. It was a very low-budget affair. They didn't even have a finale.

No Finale

If I were dying, or if I were convinced
I were dying soon, say within a year, if
I were told so by doctors, I would write
a bunch of poems out of my nervousness
and my love for being here. They would be
what I saw on walks and times I would spend
on the phone with my granddaughter remembering
when we went to the Shrine Circus, and Julio
tried the triple and missed, and there was no
finale. They just announced—when we all
expected there to be something else, at least
a parade of clowns and elephants and jungle-ladies
riding by—"Thank you for coming folks. Let's
hear it for the Shrine Circus!" But we have more
than memories. We have polaroids. Briny took
them, of brightly lit jugglers and the little girl
acrobat. She'd look through the camera hole
and then look up and snap it, but when she looked
up, the camera would tilt a little down, so
we have a number of photographs of circus dirt
with part of a spotlight circle at the top.

*I can imagine her reading that poem long after you're
gone and reliving the day at the circus with you. I like the*

idea of putting poems in the family album, like messages in a bottle. Does she write poetry herself?

You bet she does. In the first grade they had one assignment to rewrite "Little Miss Muffett." And this is what she put. It's just brilliant:

Little Miss Muffett

> Little Miss Muffett sat on the rug
> eating her chicken and licorice.
> Along came a ant and bit her

Isn't that great? "Along came a ant and bit her." That off-rhyme of "licorice and bit her." Just unbelievable.

You'll surely bring her here to the poetry festival next time.

Of course. Here's another one I wrote about her.

Justice

> Getting undressed for her bath,
> lying on her back on the bed, kicking
> and twisting her underwear off, down
> to one foot aloft twirling the cotton

pants around, she says, "I've got
underwear flags of justice."

*Don't you wonder how a child's mind puts together a
phrase like "underwear flags of justice"? I try to eavesdrop on
my own grandchildren's conversations, just to hear the fresh
play of words. But let's talk about the grown-up task of writ-
ing poetry. When you want to turn ordinary personal experi-
ence into a poem, how do you work to avoid banality? What
about the rhythm, structure, and language truly make it a
poem?*

How to avoid banality is the problem. How to make
the ordinary *glow* in a poem. In "No Finale" I took two
seemingly opposite things and put them together: my
imagined death and the circus, tawdry event though it
be. Now, a friend of mine, Jim Kilgo, had recently
been diagnosed with cancer. It was easy to put myself
in his position, of being told I was terminal. He's fine,
it turns out, but I was interested in how such news
might affect my writing. This poem claims that it
would make each moment more precious, especially
moments with Briny, which are already pretty spectac-
ularly lit for me. I brought a cheap Polaroid camera
and lots of film to the circus, and she began experi-
menting with it. Those are the elements from actual
life that went into the poem.

But what turns your account of those elements into a poem?

Partially, it's the work with sound, the fooling sleights of tongue like "Julio tried the triple and missed." Very tasty. Or, "we have a number of photographs of circus dirt," which is literally what we got when my granddaughter pointed the camera at the floor. The poem works in a lighthearted way, but it is serious too. It shows there is no finale to this fragile string of moments. I hope the poem locates us in the human circus, somewhere between spotlight and dust, waving snapshot moments. I hope "No Finale" makes the ordinary seem ecstatic.

Your poems create that effect on listeners. There's a musical quality about them. When you speak that line "Julio tried the triple and missed," the association of sound and rhythm sings in my ear. You work hard to get the form right.

Rumi says that "form is ecstatic!" Just being here now, treating this moment as revelation.

But how do you approach translating his thirteenth-century idiom into modern dress?

I try to bring some of the same slightly fancy, elegant touches to a basically conversational American idiom. I'm told that's how he sounds in Persian, colloquial and majestic, which ties in with what I was saying about his message: each moment solid and actual, yet numinous, shot through with divine light and guidance. He says, "When someone bumps against you in the street, don't react with irritation. Everyone is careening around in this surprise." He sees that we're all drunk with being sentient. I take the liberty of rephrasing the stagger of the drunk into an ecstatic careening, lost in wonder. There are associations with drunkenness now, the addiction and the violence, that I feel I have to rework.

Can you say more about what it is in the form *of the language that makes it a poem?*

I don't want to get too solemn about the terms *form* and *poem*. If it has soundwork going on and if it resonates in your body, I'd say it's close to poetry. And I love a deep playfulness.

What do you mean by soundwork?

It is just being conscious of clusters of echoic vowels and consonants. Being conscious of the way language tastes and how it sounds coming through the ear.

"Drink deep, or taste not the Pierian spring." I remember that from an undergraduate class many, many years ago. Alexander Pope was the professor's favorite. What can you say about how the imagination makes such connections?

The way images and rhythms and sound clusters work on us and through us is complicated and hidden deep in the DNA. There's an innate, mysterious core to poetic talent, a genius that can't be explained, which doesn't mean we aren't *aware* of it. We *hear* it, and we can celebrate it. The thing is to just sit, or walk around, and fiddle with language, listen to language, and see what turns up. Let yourself be open. I like "form" that feels left open.

With no finale!

That's it.

Which do you prefer, writing your own poetry about the people, places, and experiences you know best, or translating Rumi?

I like both. But with Rumi I have to try to disappear. With my own poems, I have to try to get my personality and my delights and my shame all into the poem.

I've heard you say that silence, friendship, and perhaps music live nearer to reality. What is that reality? And why do silence, friendship, and music take us closer to it?

Mystical poetry, the kind that Rumi writes, is trying to examine who we really are. Am I this person born in Chattanooga who grew up, had two sons, and got divorced and now has a grandchild and will eventually die and be buried in a graveyard like this one we're sitting in, or am I something else? Rumi said to his friend Shams, "When I see you, it is not so much your physical shape, but the company of two riders, your pure-fire devotion, and your love for the one who teaches you." Rather than seeing an old man, he sees the magnificent friendship of two riders. It's a way of saying, "We're more than what we see." He's trying to get us to feel the vastness of our true identities, which is not anything you know with your mind. It's more like the sense you might get walking into a cathedral, of the truth of your own inner space, what Jesus referred to when he said, "The kingdom of God is within you." The Rumi poems inhabit that area. It may be the *purpose* of ecstatic poetry to guide us into that place of consciousness where music and silence and friendship go more easily than language.

Yes, but in poetry it's the play of language that begins the imaginative transformation of reality. When I'm listening to you I'm not concerned with the meaning of the words, as such.

You want to feel a poem, don't you?

Sure. That's how I experience your Rumi translations. I can take one of his poems home with me without having memorized it.

His were spontaneous poems. They were *spoken* in the moment. Sometimes as a teaching, sometimes for pure celebration. Students took them down, and later he evidently did some revision. At one time, though, he said, "Don't save these songs. Don't worry about writing them down. We have fallen into the place where everything is music." And that's what this festival makes me feel—the interconnectedness of people and poems. It's amazing that so many people can be genuinely excited about fooling with words. You listen to the young people, some of them just high school kids, trying to get into phrasing, getting the words right to express what it feels like to be themselves. A gathering of people and poets is mostly a delight with language. And that's what poetry is, a delight with language. It's very hard work, the creative process of getting to the right words, the right construction, the depth of thought and feeling that turns a jumble of words into poetry.

What do you tell young people about that hard work? How does one begin to go about it?

I can only tell them how I did it. I just kept a notebook, starting when I was about twelve, and I wrote down words that I loved the taste of, words such as *azalea*, or for some reason *halcyon*, the bird that calms the wind and water while it nests on the sea. And odd words—odd for a twelve-year-old—like *jejune*, which means "dull, intellectually empty." I was a collector of odd words. And of images, too. I remember an image of a boy stirring a spiderweb with a stick. I don't know why, it stuck with me. It's a fascination or obsession with images and with the taste of words, language that is delicious to the mouth. I didn't do anything with the notebooks for a long time. I kept the lists of words and images and I didn't start putting them into poems until I was in graduate school and then I would look for images that helped me understand my own life. There's a Rumi poem—it's one of my favorites—that touches on what we're talking about.

> Time's knife slides from the sheath,
> as a fish from where it swims.
>
> Being closer and closer is the desire
> of the body. Don't wish for union!

There's a closeness beyond that. Why
would God want a second God? Fall in

love in such a way that it frees you
from any connecting. Love is the soul's

light, the taste of morning, no *me*, no
we, no claim of *being*. These words

are the smoke the fire gives off as it
absolves its defects, as eyes in silence,

tears, face. Love cannot be said.

What do you like about that poem?

That it's trying to do something impossible. The
poet's trying to say what love is with all these contradic-
tory things, and then he admits at the end that love can-
not be said. That's the reality. He wants us to point
toward what cannot be said.

*This is the Sufi notion of mystical union: "When the soul
lies down in that grass the world is too full to talk about ideas,
language, even the phrase 'each other' doesn't make any
sense."*

Yes! There's another Rumi line that I wish everyone could say to someone in their life, "I see my beauty in you."

I see my beauty in you. I become
a mirror that cannot close its eyes

to your longing. My eyes wet with
yours in the early light. My mind

every moment giving birth, always
conceiving, always in the ninth

month, always the come-point. How
do I stand this? We become these

words we say, a wailing sound moving
out into the air. These thousands of

worlds that rise from nowhere, how
does your face contain them? I'm

a fly in your honey, then closer, a
moth caught in flame's allure, then

empty sky stretched out in homage.

You've spent so much of your time now in the company of a poet who's been dead seven hundred years. What is it about him that holds you?

He was known as a "heartmaster." The work of his religious community was to open the heart to that mystery of union.

Which can include the kinship between grandfather and grandchild, perhaps?

Oh, yes.

But even Rumi tired of poetry . . . sometimes.

But you have to understand why. He grew tired of love poems because he wanted love, tired of God-poems because he wanted the Presence. In one of my favorite poems by Rumi, poems are the jars.

> Jars of springwater are not enough
> anymore. Take us down to the river!
>
> The face of peace, the sun itself.
> No more the slippery cloudlike moon.

Give us one clear morning after another
and the one whose work remains unfinished,

who *is* our work as we diminish, idle,
though occupied, empty, and open.

"Empty, and open." Ready to receive.

That's it. Poetry helps your psyche become a guest-
house of emotions.

LORNA DEE CERVANTES

SOMETIMES, WHEN SHE is reading her poetry aloud, Lorna Dee Cervantes disappears into the words. Her dark eyes close, her head tilts back, the long, black hair falls across her shoulders like a shaman's shawl, and she seems transported to a faraway place. The audience is borne away with her. Two rows of older teenagers sit directly in front of her, practically under the lectern, their imaginations fastened to hers by rivets of images and metaphors. Cervantes is reading a poem she has dedicated to one Nathan Trujillo, discovered frozen to death in a public restroom in Boulder, Colorado, and identified only as a derelict. The young people in my sight are suburban, favored. For this moment they have entered a world that is light-years beyond their experience, but not beyond their capacity to feel. They listen to this woman tell *how she walked "like a child of a maid" past "the open places, graves, the cemetery gate—the only one we're allowed to pass without eviction." At the poem's end she tells them, almost in a whisper, "I'd say I was a derelict, I was a derelict's kid." As she turns to leave the stage, the audience begins to applaud. The young people I have been watching do not stir, not one of them. They are still in that faraway place, and I am not sure they know how to get back. They have touched, and been touched by, the reality of another life.*

I know you to be a private person who cherishes the time alone it takes to compose. Does it then take a lot of chutzpah to get up at a festival like this and read your poetry?

Yes, but not as much as it takes to put your poems in an envelope and to send them out, to call yourself a writer. I think a lot of my writing is a result of my being so shy when I was a child. When you grow up as a Chican-India in a barrio in a Mexican neighborhood in California, part of the welfare class, you're not expected to speak, much less write, or call yourself a writer. They didn't teach poetry in the barrio schools. I thought poetry had died out a hundred years ago. So my own lack of self-confidence was my biggest obstacle to taking that tremendous step you have to take in order to say, "I am a writer." And when I did start writing, I kept my poems to myself, stuck in a notebook. I didn't show anyone.

When did the idea strike, that you could write?

I was eight years old. My brother was always singing songs and looking at songbooks. I thought poems were songs for people with bad voices. And my brother always assured me that's what I had. I started writing for the same reason I breathe—because I had to. I heard voices. I would hear a rhyme. When I was a child I was always making up songs. The first poem I wrote was to "Greensleeves"—I just loved the tune. And suddenly this language erupted and I heard these words and I wrote them down, and they pleased me.

My brother dropped out of school and became a janitor in a junior high school. And he used to borrow books from the library. He did it alphabetically, and he got all the way to the *D*'s before they found out and he lost his job. By then, thanks to him, I was going to the library. I was a street kid by day and by night I was a library kid. The library—it's now the Museum of Art in San Jose—was open until 11:30 at night. I would go there and scan the shelves alphabetically. I was drawn to anyone with a female name, with a Latino or Spanish name. There were very, very few. But as a teenager I discovered African American poetry. Gwendolyn Brooks was the first.

Then Phillis Wheatley. I really identified with this slave woman writing poetry to assert and affirm her humanity. Suddenly my eyes were open to history. There was a whole explosion of African-American women poets—Audre Lorde, Nikki Giovanni, June Jordan. I have a poem in my head that's going to take me years to write down. Its working title is "On Thanking Black Muses." I owe them, because poetry really changed my life, saved it. I mean that literally.

You're alive now, because of poetry?

Oh, yes. Right after my first book was accepted by the publisher, I moved to Provincetown, and I was unpacking all my things and I found this foldout from my middle school class. Pictures of all the kids in that class. It hadn't been all that long—I was about twenty-three or twenty-four—and I looked at those pictures and I thought: Wow! He's dead, died driving drunk. She's dead, her boyfriend killed her. This couple's dead, overdosed on barbiturates. He's dead, killed in prison. And on and on. I realized that almost fifty percent of my junior high school class was dead. I could have been one of them.

You wrote a poem about one of your classmates—"For Virginia Chavez."

She's still alive, I think. She's somewhere out there. But yes, that poem is about a real person, a real event. She was my best friend, two years older than I, and she lived across the street and had already dropped out of school at fourteen and had three children. So I begin the poem:

For Virginia Chavez

It was never in the planning,
in the life we thought
we'd live together, two fast
women living cheek to cheek,
still tasting the dog's
breath of boys in our testy
new awakening.
We were never the way
they had it planned.
Their wordless tongues we stole
and tasted the power
that comes of that.
We were never what they wanted
but we were bold. We could take
something of life and not
give it back. We could utter
the rules, mark the lines
and cross them ourselves—we two

women using our fists, we thought,
our wits, our tunnels. They were such
dumb hunks of warm fish
swimming inside us,
but this was love,
we knew, love, and that was all
we were ever offered.

You were always alone
so another lonely life
wouldn't matter.
In the still house
your mother left you,
when the men were gone
and the television droned
into test patterns, with our cups
of your mother's whiskey
balanced between the brown thighs
creeping out of our shorts, I read
you the poems of Lord Byron, Donne,
the Brownings: all about love,
explaining the words
before realizing that you knew
all that the kicks in your belly
had to teach you. You were proud
of the woman blooming out of your
fourteen lonely years, but you cried

when you read that poem I wrote you,
something about our "waning moons"
and the child in me
I let die that summer.

In the years that separate,
in the tongues that divide
and conquer, in the love
that was a language
in itself, you never spoke,
never regret. Even
that last morning
I saw you with blood
in your eyes, blood
on your mouth, the blood
pushing out of you
in purple blossoms.

He did this.
When I woke, the kids
were gone. They told me
I'd never get them back.

With our arms holding
each other's waists, we walked
the waking streets
back to your empty flat,

ignoring the horns and catcalls
behind us, ignoring what
the years had brought between us:
my diploma and the bare bulb
that always lit your bookless room.

One of the last times I saw her, she'd been beaten by her boyfriend. He was physically abusing her children, and because of that they took her three kids away from her. I can still see her. If it hadn't been for poetry, books, the library, that could have been me. That's what I mean about poetry saving my life. Why didn't I end up like that? I ran in a gang when I was that age. The women were much more violent than the boys— and I say women, because at fourteen, fifteen years old, we were women. Very, very intelligent women; you've got to be sly to get by in the streets. They were smart. I'm not any better or smarter, any wiser, any more talented. It's like the trauma that someone experiences when the plane goes down and the person sitting next to you dies and you survive and you think—Why me? Who am I?

You end the poem with the image of the "bookless room." You've made sure your rooms are full of books. Perhaps they are the answer to your question.

It's an irony. My mother loved poetry. She would play records of actresses reading Elizabeth Barrett Browning, and Poe—she loved Edgar Allan Poe. She would read "Annabel Lee" and "The Raven." But the books I told you my brother brought home from the library I had to read in the closet. I would drive my mother crazy if I sat around reading books. She was very, very bitter, you see. My parents were divorced, and my mother had to raise us alone, on welfare, with just menial jobs. She was an intelligent woman who had no alternatives—nowhere to go. If she saw me reading a book, she would make me clean the toilet as punishment. She would make me clean it ten times, so that today I can clean a toilet like you wouldn't believe! My mother said to me, "This is what you have to look forward to. No one is ever going to pay you to read books. The only future you have to look forward to is being a maid, so you better make sure you are going to be the best maid possible."

But here you are, a poet!

Now, people pay me to read books. For me, poetry has been an exercise in freedom. Freedom is like a muscle—the more you exercise it, the stronger it gets. Poetry can give you a sense of choice. It's free on every level. Language and memory have no price tags on them. You have limitless choices—in form, language, subject matter—that spill over into life.

Tell me about your poem "Summer Ends Too Soon."

It is what I call an unedited poem. You may know about those exercises where everyone puts a title—just a title—on a slip of paper and drops it in a hat and then you draw out a title and you have seven minutes to write a poem about that title without revision, without editing. So this is an unedited poem. It's based on a true story about a girl, a Chican-India in the barrio in Denver, who wrote poetry at the age of seventeen in the same way I wrote poetry. Right around her high school graduation, she hung herself from a tree.

Summer Ends Too Soon

Was the last she said. Beautiful
María, Ave María. María dodging
father's fists—and his. María praying
under the table. María crooning pain
songs in the bathroom. María combing
his sludge out of her hair. María
serving masters. Seventeen year

old María. María, your Lady
of the Kept Secret. María dancing
to his temper. María washing
her panties in the toilet. Two
days after graduation, María
swaying from the limb. María,
sweet purple fruit of his sin.
Ave María.

When I see the impact such a poem has on the audience here—you've wrapped them in a virtual cocoon—I remember something Stanley Kunitz once told me. He said, "Poetry explores depths of thought and feeling that civilization requires for its survival." What have you learned about mining the depths of language and memory that evoke such feelings?

Things come to me, they speak to me. Stanley Kunitz has had an enormous impact on my life. He once said that poetry is only half language, the other half is a quality of perception, a function of the imagination, a particular form of paying attention. For me, it's a stilling of the self, waiting for this language to speak to me before I utter it.

Yes, but how does that happen?

You just have to read, read, read, write, write, and write. I don't know what else to say. Work is the refiner's fire.

In one of your poems you also say that work is the refuge of sadness.

Sadness overcomes us when we remember. It's better to just keep busy.

You make me think of one of your poems I especially like, called "Poet's Progress."

I'm glad you like that. A long, long time ago I came upon a poem that Sandra Cisneros had written. I found it in a magazine, and I wrote her. I published her first chapbook of poetry. And then I recently wrote this poem for her.

Poet's Progress

for Sandra Cisneros

I haven't been
much of anywhere,
books my only voyage,
crossed no bodies

of water, seen anything
other than trees change,
birds take shape—like the rare
Bee Hummingbird that once hovered
over the promise of salsa
in my garden: a fur feathered
vision from Cuba in Boulder,
a wetback, stowaway, refugee,
farther from home than me.
Now, snow spatters its foreign
starch across the lawn gone
crisp with freeze. I know
nothing tropical survives
long in this season. I pull
the last leeks from the frozen
earth, smell their slender
tubercular lives, stand
in the sleet whiteout
of December: roots
draw in, threads of relatives
expand while solitude, the core,
that slick-headed fist of self, is
cool as my dog's nose and pungent
with resistance. Now when
the red-bellied woodpecker
calls his response to a California
owl, now, when the wound

transformer in the womb
slackens, and I wait
for potential: all
the lives I have
yet to name,
all my life
I have willed into being
alive and brittle with the icy
past. And it's enough now,
listening, counting the unknown
arachnids and hormigas
who share my love of less
sweeping. For this is what
I wanted, come to, left
alone with anything
but the girlhood horrors,
the touching, the hungry
leaden meltdown of the hours.
Or the future—a round negation,
black suction of the heart's
conception. *Save me*
from a stupid life! I prayed.
Leave me anything but
a stupid life.
And that's poetry.

We're back to how poetry saved you.

Well, the poem is to Sandra, reflecting on our lives. Sandra grew up on the South Side of Chicago and I grew up in California and this poem reflects on the progression of our lives, the poet's spiritual progress or journey. At the time I wrote this poem, Sandra had just come back from Crete and had just signed a six-figure contract—her first one. I was comparing her travels—across bodies of water, which I had not done—and the poet's journey across oceans of consciousness. There is a great satisfaction that comes from being in the life that one has chosen. When I say, "Save me from a stupid life," I mean an unquestioned life, those unexamined choices that Sandra and I were both expected to make. We both chose poetry, which, to me, is the exact opposite of the stupid life.

MARK DOTY

*O*DD, *HOW YOU can hear something all your life, over and over again, enjoying it each time, but not know what it is you are enjoying, not even know it has a name. That's the way it's been with the melisma and me. I could not begin to count the times I have heard the "Hallelujah Chorus" of Handel's* Messiah, *how often I have exulted in that passage where the voices reach, hold, and repeat, and repeat, and repeat the* o *in Gloria. Glo-o-o-o-o-o-o-o-o-o-o-o-o-o-o-o-o-o-r-i-a. Whether it is performed by the noted Musica Sacra at Carnegie Hall, or by the lay choir of our local church, or by neighbors gathered in a friend's home, harmoniously celebrating the season (well, perhaps not always so harmoniously), I relish the moment it arrives, the moment of melisma. Melisma, I learned from Mark Doty, is the techni-*

cal name for what thrills my soul—a musical passage of one syllable sung over many notes, as in Gregorian chants. Because the word appears unexpectedly in Doty's "Messiah (Christmas Portions)," he alerts the audience in advance to its presence and meaning. It is the only esoteric word in a poem so otherwise evocative of the familiar that, as he reads, we are brought to laughter and tears and then to our feet, cheering. Mark Doty is often cheered when he reads, even though his poems frequently deal with life's bad news. Perhaps it is because the pleasure and pain in his poetry are so layered that, sooner or later, all of us find ourselves between his lines. Listening to his account of the voices performing the melisma—altos from the A&P, the soprano from the T-shirt shop, the neighbor fighting operatically with her girlfriend— I see in my mind's eye the choir from my youth at Central Baptist Church in Marshall, Texas. By weekday its director, Lucille Williams, was a clerk, but on Sunday mornings she cut a grand figure as she summoned from secretaries, carpenters, toolmakers, merchants, and housewives such singing as would have made celestial choristers jealous, at least of its exuberance. What I now know to have been their melismas still sound in my head, their comforting ordinariness a reminder of the unexpected glories—make that glo-o-o-o-o-ries—inherent even in imperfection. Perhaps that notice in the church bulletin was no blooper after all, the one that read, "Any member of the congregation who enjoys sinning is invited to join the choir."

This poem began in a moment of skepticism, right?

I came to this poem because I live, most of the
time, in a small town in coastal Massachusetts, and a
few years ago our local choral society decided to
mount a performance of Handel's *Messiah*. This was
an ambitious project, and a number of us felt some
trepidation about the possible results. The day of the
performance I arrived at the church just as an unbe-
lievably beautiful sunset was occurring overhead. It
seemed ironic to leave that perfectly accomplished
sunset behind and enter the chapel for a doubtful
human achievement. What happened inside brought
on this poem.

Messiah (Christmas Portions)

A little heat caught
in gleaming rags,
in shrouds of veil,
    torn and sun-shot swaddlings:

over the Methodist roof,
two clouds propose a Zion
of their own, blazing
    (colors of tarnish on copper)

against the steely close
of a coastal afternoon, December,
while under the steeple
  the Choral Society

  prepares to perform
Messiah, pouring, in their best
blacks and whites, onto the raked stage.
  Not steep, really,

  but from here,
the first pew, they're a looming
cloudbank of familiar angels:
  that neighbor who

  fights operatically
with her girlfriend, for one,
and the friendly bearded clerk
  from the post office

  —tenor trapped
in the body of a baritone? Altos
from the A&P, soprano
  from the T-shirt shop:

today they're all poise,
costume and purpose
conveying the right note
   of distance and formality.

   Silence in the hall,
anticipatory, as if we're all
about to open a gift we're not sure
   we'll like;

   how could they
compete with sunset's burnished
oratorio? Thoughts which vanish,
   when the violins begin.

   Who'd have thought
they'd be so good? *Every valley*,
proclaims the solo tenor,
   (a sleek blonde

   I've seen somewhere before
—the liquor store?) *shall be exalted*,
and in his handsome mouth the word
   is lifted and opened

   into more syllables
than we could count, central *ah*

dilated in a baroque melisma,
   liquefied; the pour

of voice seems
to *make* the unplaned landscape
the text predicts the Lord
   will heighten and tame.

This music
demonstrates what it claims:
glory shall be revealed. If art's
   acceptable evidence,

mustn't what lies
behind the world be at least
as beautiful as the human voice?
   The tenors lack confidence,

and the soloists,
half of them anyway, don't
have the strength to found
   the mighty kingdoms

these passages propose
—but the chorus, all together,
equals my burning clouds,
   and seems itself to burn,

commingled powers
deeded to a larger, centering claim.
These aren't anyone we know;
    choiring dissolves

    familiarity in an up-
pouring rush which will not
rest, will not, for a moment,
    be still.

    Aren't we enlarged
by the scale of what we're able
to desire? Everything,
    the choir insists,

    might flame;
inside these wrappings
burns another, brighter life,
    quickened, now,

    by song: hear how
it cascades, in overlapping,
lapidary waves of praise? Still time.
    Still time to change.

The applause after you finished reading that poem went on and on.

The impact an appreciative audience can have on you is amazing! One could get very used to the experience. I suspect that the poem has a particular resonance for this audience, too, because it's about coming together in community. It speaks to the power of our combined voices. And that's what happens at the Dodge Festival, all these solitudes coming together into connection.

They responded just as enthusiastically to "New Dog."

That's an excerpt from a longer sequence called "Atlantis." There are some friends who make an appearance, but the central characters in the poem are my late partner, Wally Roberts, who died of complications of AIDS in 1994, and a four-legged character— we'll let him introduce himself.

New Dog

Jimi and Tony
can't keep Dino,
their cocker spaniel;
Tony's too sick,
the daily walks

more pressure
than pleasure,
one more obligation
that can't be met.

And though we already
have a dog, Wally
wants to adopt,
wants something small
and golden to sleep
next to him and
lick his face.
He's paralyzed now
from the waist down,

whatever's ruining him
moving upward, and
we don't know
how much longer
he'll be able to pet
a dog. How many men
want another attachment,
just as they're
leaving the world?

Wally sits up nights
and says, *I'd like*

some lizards, a talking bird,
some fish. A little rat.
So after I drive
to Jimi and Tony's
in the Village and they
meet me at the door and say,
We can't go through with it,

we can't give up our dog,
I drive to the shelter
—just to look—and there
is Beau: bounding and
practically boundless,
one brass concatenation
of tongue and tail,
unmediated energy,
too big, wild,

perfect. He not only
licks Wally's face
but bathes every
irreplaceable inch
of his head, and though
Wally can no longer
feed himself he can lift
his hand, and bring it
to rest on the rough gilt

flanks when they are,
for a moment, still.
I have never seen a touch
so deliberate.
It isn't about grasping;
the hand itself seems
almost blurred now,
softened, though
tentative only

because so much will
must be summoned,
such attention brought
to the work—which is all
he is now, this gesture
toward the restless splendor,
the unruly, the golden,
the animal, the new.

What I'm writing about in this poem is a gesture made by a man in the very late moments of his life; a man who had lost the use of much of his body, who knew very well that the end was near, and who could still reach out to a new dog he could love, something he found beautiful, just to give that touch that says, "I find this world worth participating in, even though I can't stay in it." I was struck by the realization: He's the one who's dying, and if he's able to feel that way, that tenderness towards experience, I have to find that responsiveness, too. No matter what you may lose, it is possible to respond with tenderness.

This was the early nineties, remember, and there were so many people dying—my own partner and many friends around us. It was before the advent of the new medications, which have made it possible for some people to live much longer, healthier lives. This was a moment of profound hopelessness. Our lives had been scoured by the AIDS epidemic. Nothing had so inscribed and transformed my own experience as that whole constellation of events. I realized that all we had was our ability to take care of each other, to stand with each other. We had our dreams, we had the ways in which we negotiated privately with loss. It was imperative, it seemed to me, that we see ourselves as being part of a community of caretakers, dreamers, and mortal beings.

How do you take something so deeply felt, so inaudible as grief, and find the language that brings an audience into the experience?

This is the place where the craft of poetry is paramount: the love of the sheer physical pleasures of language, its sonics, its textures, its rhythms. I might write a poem which begins in raw and inchoate feeling. Most of my poems do begin that way. They come tumbling out of me, but that's a cry, not a poem. An unshaped utterance is not a poem. I let the words flow, I let them come out wherever they will. Then I have to stand back from them and begin to shape the language so that the poem becomes available to another person. You must stand at a distance from yourself and apply all the resources you can muster to the raw stuff of experience. It's not easy, especially if you're writing about the hardest things in the world, which is what poetry must do ultimately. Frankly, I have felt very grateful during those times of new grief to have the long habit of discipline so necessary to writing. Everything else might be falling apart, but here is something over which I had some control. I've devoted my life to trying to get words to behave in ways that will influence, affect, please, and involve readers in a way which will somehow do justice to the complexity and beauty of reality. So there I was overwhelmed by emotion, but the other side of me—the technician, the maker—could take over, and make a vessel which at least tried to contain all that feeling. No matter what, that side of me is ready to go to work on the materials of experience.

It's uncanny, the power of poetry to transform an experience.

One of poetry's great powers is its preservative ability to take a moment in time and make an attempt to hold it. Yeats said a great and terrifying thing: "All that is personal soon rots unless it is packed in ice or salt." Of course the ice and salt he meant was the power of form, the preservative element of language, which can hold a moment from the past, allow us to return to it, and allow us to give it to someone else. That element allows you as a reader to enter imaginatively into the poem, be part of it yourself, and bring your losses to bear upon it—so that the poem becomes a kind of meeting ground between us. Art has that power. What the poem makes is a version of a moment, a replica, a touchstone—something to keep, and to give away. We shape a poem in order to let it go; the process of crafting the poem, of trying to get everything from line to sonic texture to each individual word just right involves standing back and gaining a greater degree of distance from what we've said. A good poem may begin in self-expression, but it ends as art, which means it isn't really for the writer anymore but for the reader who steps into and makes the experience of the poem her or his own. Therein lies the marvel: The poet's little limited life becomes larger because readers enter into it. Wally really is gone, and yet he—and he and I together—figure into the imaginative lives of readers. That's an extraordinary thing, that something as small as a poem extends our lives.

*I see it happen at poetry events. Poets create community,
like the singers in your choir did in that church.*

I find great hope in that sense of connection with other
people, the possibility that the worst experiences might be
transformed into a place where we might meet and stand
together. It happens. So often after a reading someone
will come up to me, someone who has just heard a poem
or read one of my books, and say, "You said how I felt."
We need that, I think, as a species; we are the creatures
which represent, which long to be represented. As a
reader, I am always looking to recognize my own experi-
ence in others' work. That's one of the things I love most
about literature, coming across a passage which says what
I know but have never been able to say.

*Every poet I talk to acknowledges a debt to the work of
other poets, living and dead.*

One of my favorite poems in the world is Rainer
Maria Rilke's "Archaic Torso of Apollo," which is about
encountering a beautiful, ruined statue in the Louvre,
an antique Greek figure which is now headless. Despite
the fact that the figure is broken, Rilke looks at it and
sees how incredibly alive it is. This fragment of art
somehow seems more alive than the speaker in the

poem; even in its incomplete state it seems to say, "Look how much is possible. Look what you could be." I certainly recognize that experience, of feeling humbled and challenged by art, but no one has ever said it as clearly and resonantly as Rilke did.

And his poem inspired one of your own.

Yes. I also wrote about encountering a fragment. Rilke's poem begins, in Robert Bly's translation, "We do not know what this fantastic head was like . . . " I've borrowed that line, which you will see in another version a few lines into the poem. The poem also refers to the great Renaissance painter Giotto, whose frescoes make use of this sock-you-in-the-eyes blue which represents heaven. It is one of that intensity and power.

A Green Crab's Shell

> Not, exactly, green:
> closer to bronze
> preserved in kind brine,
>
> something retrieved
> from a Greco-Roman wreck,
> patinated and oddly

muscular. We cannot
know what his fantastic
legs were like—

though evidence
suggests eight
complexly folded

scuttling works
of armament, crowned
by the foreclaws'

gesture of menace
and power. A gull's
gobbled the center,

leaving this chamber
—size of a demitasse—
open to reveal

a shocking, Giotto blue.
Though it smells
of seaweed and ruin,

this little traveling case
comes with such lavish lining!
Imagine breathing

surrounded by
the brilliant rinse
of summer's firmament.

What color is
the underside of skin?
Not so bad, to die,

if we could be opened
into *this*—
if the smallest chambers

of ourselves,
similarly,
revealed some sky.

*To what extent do you think your poetry is self-revelatory?
You draw on your own experience so often in the poems I've
read.*

For a lot of my life I was not particularly confident or
authoritative about myself. My father was an army engi-
neer, and we moved all the time. I was a bookish kid, a
gay kid. I was the sissy who would hide under the steps
to the library and read while the rest of the class was
playing soccer. One of the results of living on the mar-
gin like that, feeling like an outsider, is the sense of

wanting connection to other people, other lives. You discover yourself paying attention to the signals around you to see what's going on beneath the surface.

Let me put it this way. I had a sense that what people could see of me, and the life I was living inside me, were very different things. Here on the outside was this unhappy, disconnected kid who didn't know what to do with himself. And here on the inside was a kind of golden interior life, which had to do with the world of books and daydreams and the imagination. And you realize that if that's true of yourself, then maybe it's true of other people, too—that what you can see on the surface is not what's lingering beneath. Perhaps my impulse to write has to do with that desire to meet, to make a space, if you will, where the interiority of the writer and the inner life of the reader might have a sort of conversation.

When did you know you wanted to be a poet?

From the time I could read I was always writing something, but it wasn't poetry. In high school I began to keep a journal—not a diary, because I was bored just writing down what happened to me. I was never very good at that. But I kept a record of impressions, images, daydreams—bits and pieces that would have felt incomprehensible to anyone else. Maybe I wanted it that way; I wanted to hide them. But I felt I was paying attention to my inner life, and that little space, that notebook, became the space where I could represent the parts of me that other people couldn't see. Then I began to shape and play around with them because at the same time I was falling in love with real poems. I loved Tolkien's *Lord of the Rings* with the little songs the characters sang, and the poems of Federico García Lorca, which are so saturated in color and image and are so beautifully and dreamily musical. Those seemed to me an evidence of something—a movement of spirit that I didn't see much reflected in the life around me. I could hear myself saying, "That's where I want to go. That's what I want to find in myself." I gradually began to play with these fragments and make them into poems.

I was very lucky when I was sixteen to meet a poet, a wonderful teacher named Richard Shelton, who began to read my work and to meet with me every now and then to give me suggestions about what to read. He very wisely didn't offer a lot of suggestions on my fledgling, awful poems. He would just say, "Write another one," or, "Look at this, look at what this writer has done." Most important, he was an example of an adult who organized his life around a passion. He said, "This is what matters to me; no matter what, I will live in a way that honors what people create." I didn't know that was possible. One thing I love about this festival is seeing the thousands of high school kids trooping in here excited about the possibility of other ways to live, about the choice that poets make to do something difficult, unlikely, a little out of the mainstream.

I can see some of these kids imagining themselves as Mark Doty reading their poems from that stage.

The response of the audience is thrilling for me on a couple of levels. I think most of us never really believe we're going to have readers. Poems are always made in solitude, and it's always startling when they move from that privacy into community. Then it's thrilling in another way, too. When I was a teenager, I never saw a self-identified adult gay person. I didn't even know that was a possibility. And I felt utterly alone, and had periods of feeling profoundly suicidal, feeling there's no way I can live in accordance with my desires. What on earth am I going to do, I wondered—spend my life in hiding? without a sense of love and connection? It would have made a great difference to meet some adults who were confident in themselves, who could say, "You'll be all right. There is a life you can live. There are possibilities for you." I don't think that's the primary work of poetry; that's not *why* I write. But it is deeply satisfying to me to be able to stand up and be visible, to be recognized for who I am.

So why do you write?

You've heard this before! Because I don't have a choice. Because it is the way I know what I think and feel. And I find that if I don't give shape to my experience in language, if I don't spend time in the crafting and honing of that experience in words, I don't feel real to myself. It's as if the layer of experience which completes myself is the act of writing, the act of naming what I've known.

In one of my favorite poems you let your dog do the naming.

Well, I had to let Beau have his say. This is a poem that began when I was invited to contribute to an anthology called *Unleashed.* All the poems had to be in the voice of the writer's dog. And I thought, No, I'd never write a poem that way. About a week later, Beau and I were out for a walk in the woods, and I started picking up these signals—a kind of subtle transmission taking place. What can I say? He's fond of puns. He wanted to dictate this sonnet.

Golden Retrievals

Fetch? Balls and sticks capture my attention
seconds at a time. Catch? I don't think so.
Bunny, tumbling leaf, a squirrel who's—oh
joy—actually scared. Sniff the wind, then

I'm off again: muck, pond, ditch, residue
of any thrillingly dead thing. And you?
Either you're sunk in the past, half our walk,
thinking of what you never can bring back,

or else you're off in some fog concerning
—tomorrow, is that what you call it? My work:
to unsnare time's warp (and woof!), retrieving,
my haze-headed friend, you. This shining bark,

a Zen master's bronzy gong, calls you here,
entirely, now: bow-wow, bow-wow, bow-wow.

Deborah Garrison

*T*HE SIGHTINGS BEGAN *early in the year. On the subway, during rush hour, a young woman balances her briefcase on her knees with one hand and with the other holds the book close to her face; the car is packed, but she might as well be sitting in a nunnery, sheltered by silence. In a busy bagel shop another young woman sits eating her sesame and cream cheese, the book open on the counter, propped against her purse. Deborah Garrison's* A Working Girl Can't Win *has just been favorably reviewed—not once but twice—in* The New York Times, *and working women throughout the city have discovered a new heroine, a veteran at age thirty-two, from the front lines of the office wars, reporting in a voice sometimes defiant and tinged with sarcasm but humorous, too, and sweetened by tender longing. Now, some months*

later, Deborah Garrison is the youngest of the featured poets at the Dodge Festival. She has been introduced as a senior editor at The New Yorker, *but it is her reading, not her résumé, that has the audience—a mixed group, male and female, tousle-haired teenagers and balding septuagenarians—as enthralled as the intent subway rider or the devotee at the bagel bar.*

Let's start with the poem that hits like pure caffeine.

Okay.

Please Fire Me

Here comes another alpha male,
and all the other alphas
are snorting and pawing,
kicking up puffs of acrid dust

while the silly little hens
clatter back and forth
on quivering claws and raise
a titter about the fuss.

Here comes another alpha male—
a man's man, a dealmaker,

holds tanks of liquor,
charms them pantsless at lunch:

I've never been sicker.
Do I have to stare into his eyes
and sympathize? If I want my job
I do. Well I think I'm through

with the working world,
through with warming eggs
and being Zenlike in my detachment
from all things Ego.

I'd like to go
somewhere else entirely,
and I don't mean
Europe.

The audience was delighted with that last line—"I'd like to go / somewhere else entirely, / and I don't mean / Europe." But we want to know, if not Europe, where?

It's a strange line, isn't it? Sometimes you don't know where a line comes from. I wasn't sure why I mentioned Europe, but after I wrote it down I couldn't change it. I couldn't find something that made more obvious sense. I think the idea is that "Europe" refers to an even more old-fashioned culture, one where alpha males have been around a long time, so if I'm here in America complaining about alpha males, I certainly wouldn't want to go to Europe, which is even further behind us in that respect. And the other sort of joke at the end there is that if I want to get away, I don't mean just to another country, I mean to another planet. I had thought of titling the poem "Goodbye to This Planet." I want a completely different existence that's out there somewhere.

What is it about alpha males that makes you want to leave "here" altogether—to be in another world, another reality?

They take up a lot of space. And they like to hear themselves talk.

Yet you have this talent for seeing another side to them. Your poem "The Boss" led me to wonder about the hidden side of people like him with whom I've worked.

The Boss

A firecracker, even after middle age
set in, a prince of repression
in his coat and tie, with cynical words

for everything dear to him.
Once I saw a snapshot of the house
he lives in, its fence painted

white, the flowers a wife
had planted leaning into the frame
on skinny stalks, shaking little pom-poms

of color, the dazzle all
accidental, and I felt
a hot, corrective

sting: our lives would never
intersect. At some point
he got older, trimmer, became

the formidable man around the office.
His bearing upright, what hair he has
silver and smooth, he shadows my doorway,

jostling the change in his pocket—
milder now, and mildly vexed.
The other day he asked what on earth

was wrong with me, and sat me down
on his big couch, where I cried
for twenty minutes straight,

snuffling, my eyeliner
betraying itself in the stained
tears. Impossible to say I was crying

because he had asked. He passed
tissues, at ease with the fearsome
womanly squall that made me alien

even to myself. No, it didn't make him
squirm. Across his seventy years,
over his glasses, he eyed me kindly,

and I thought what countless scenes
of tears, of love revealed,
he must have known.

All our relationships have many sides—at the
office, in our marriages. This is partly what poetry is
about: pulling back from where you are, so that
instead of feeling lost in the mire you find a way to
describe that world and, in doing so, you are lifted a
little bit out of it. Marge Piercy has said that you can
be happy writing a poem about being dumped! Now
that's a funny and smart way of putting it—that you
can construct your experience in this artful way, in a
way that's aesthetically and emotionally satisfying, so

that getting dumped becomes completely secondary
and the humor, the sorrow, whatever the emotion, is
mediated by poetry.

*I like that notion of poetry as constructing one's experience
in an artful way. In the workshop you turned the experience
of a kiss into a poem that had the students doing a double take
at the end.*

A Kiss

It was not like everyone had said.
Not like being needed,
or needing; not desperate;
it did not whisper
that I'd come to harm. I didn't lose

my head. No, I was not
going to leap from a great
height and flap
my wings.
It was in fact

the opposite of flying:
it contained the wish
to be toppled, to be on the floor,

the ground, anywhere I might
lie down. . . .

On my back, and you on me.
Do you mind?
Not like having a conversation, exactly,
though not unlike telling
and being told—

What?
That I was like a woman admitting
there was a part of herself she didn't know?
There was a part of myself.
I didn't know.

An introduction,
then, to the woman I was like,
at least as long as you kissed me.
Now that's a long time,
at least a couple of women ago.

When you're fifteen or sixteen, you're thinking a lot
about kissing. But what struck me is how many different
responses there were to the meaning of the kiss. One
young man said he thought the narrator was "defiant."
Another student said she thought the poem was about
memory. And she was right on. I didn't set out just to

describe a kiss as experienced in the moment. I wanted to give the poem an extra layer, which is what makes a poem a poem. If I had merely described a kiss and how it feels, I'd be lucky to get a B+. So in that last line—"Now that's a long time, / at least a couple of women ago"—I tried to suggest the bite, the extra overlay, of a remembered experience.

Have you made your peace with the fact that once you finish a poem and you let it out, others will make what they will of it?

It's a paradox, isn't it? You create poetry when you're alone, it's a very private thing, and you're not really thinking of who your audience is. You sit there in the middle of the night, trying to figure out the form it should take, looking for words that connect at some basic level to each other—a very solitary experience occurring in your head—but somewhere in the back of your mind, you know the reason you're doing this, the reason for the struggle, is that you have to invite other people into the experience you are writing about. You're trying to communicate something. But the first criterion is for it to work on the page, right there in front of you.

When did you begin to do that? When did poetry first engage you?

In the ninth grade a marvelous English teacher gave us "Thirteen Ways of Looking at a Blackbird" by Wallace Stevens, and she asked us to write a poem about thirteen ways of looking at something. I did an incredibly corny one. I wrote about thirteen ways of looking at a rainbow. One of the images I chose was a classmate's striped T-shirt that was lying in a puddle on the locker room floor, and I felt excited about this discovery—that this T-shirt with its multicolored stripes was a rainbow. And just the idea of thirteen ways of looking at anything was thrilling to me. So I began to write poetry—not very good poetry—when I was fourteen or fifteen, and then in college I was introduced to the Romantic poets. I think up until then I had thought I would be a doctor, like my father. But I was pulled more and more into poetry and away from science. After school, I fell into editing as my main-line work, and poetry for me was a kind of moonlighting. I would lie awake in bed at night and an idea would come to me. Or after work, when I'd finished at the office, before I had to go home and cook dinner, I would try out some ideas on the typewriter there. Sometimes months would go by and I wouldn't write a thing, because, well, life is so seductive for a young person living in New York. In the end, though, it didn't matter, since so much of what was happening around me and to me in the office became the stuff of these poems.

The audience really liked "An Idle Thought." That one wasn't about the office.

I'm not sure they believed me when I said that I wrote that poem before anyone had ever heard of Monica Lewinsky. But it really was about me, or about getting married at twenty-one.

An Idle Thought

I'm never going to sleep
with Martin Amis
or anyone famous.
At twenty-one I scotched
my chance to be
one of the seductresses
of the century,
a vamp on the rise through the ranks
of literary Gods and military men,
who wouldn't stop at the President:
she'd take the Pentagon by storm
in halter dress and rhinestone extras,
letting fly the breasts that shatter
crystal—then dump him, too,
and break his power-broker heart.

Such women are a breed apart.
I'm the type
who likes to cook—no,
really likes it; does the bills;
buys towels and ties;
closes her eyes during kisses:
a true first wife.

The seductress when she's fifty
nobody misses, but a first wife
always knows she's first,
and the second (if he leaves me
when he's forty-five) won't forget me
either. The mention of my name,
the sight of our son—his and mine—
will make her tense; despite
perfected bod, highlighted hair
and hip career, she'll always fear
that way back there
he loved me more
and better simply
for being first.

But ho:
the fantasy's unfair to him,
who picked me young and never tried

another. The only woman he's ever left
was his mother.

*That's one I enjoyed reading aloud to myself last evening.
The rhythm and structure of the last stanza roll off the
tongue. But I'm intrigued that the first poems you read at the
festival were not your own.*

Since I'm such a newcomer, I thought I should share
my experience of reading other poets and how they
drew me into poetry when I was myself a teenager. I
read some poems by the British poet Philip Larkin. His
tone is very conversational and irreverent. His work
meant a lot to me when I was in high school and has
ever since. I was able to talk to the students at the work-
shop about how poetry is not just formal aesthetics but
a conversation between two people, between Galway
Kinnell or Philip Larkin and a schoolgirl in Ann Arbor,
Michigan.

*That's a generous tribute to your elders. Are you aware of
being the youngest poet performing at this festival?*

Yes, and I can't tell you what it means to be around
people who are legends to me—Galway Kinnell and
Amiri Baraka and Adrienne Rich. Kinnell's *Selected*

Poems was the first book I bought with my own money as a high school student. I took my baby-sitting money, went into the Borders in Ann Arbor (this was before it became a national chain), I went up to the poetry shelf, and his was the first book I picked out. His language was about the world that I wanted to understand and be part of. I felt like someone was speaking directly to me, or trying to.

Your own work has achieved a very conversational tone— like the talk around an office watercooler. Hearing it is easy on the ear, but composing it, I know, is a very difficult process. Is it possible to break that process down for an outsider to see its parts?

I do like poems that capture the way people really talk. Robert Frost said something to the effect that gossip has a wonderful intimacy and actuality, and that the effect of actuality and intimacy is the greatest aim an artist can have. The tricky part is, What makes it poetry? If your tone is conversational, as I work hard to make mine, and you use everyday language and syntax, what makes it poetry? Let's say I want to write a poem in which I describe what it's like when my husband is out of the house and I'm roaming around the apartment without him, enjoying myself. I can sit here and describe that to you in a conversation. But to take something very natural and reconstruct it in a poem, and maybe find a rhyme in it, and words that connect below the surface, and still have it all come out sounding as natural as the experience, almost as natural as our conversation— there's the struggle. And I find it very hard. I have to revise and revise. I keep repeating and retyping the poem over and over again making tiny changes.

So you do this editing on a word processor?

No, a typewriter. The problem with a word processor—at least for me it's a problem—is that if you want to change a word, it's too easy. You don't retype the whole poem. You just go in—it's like a heat-seeking missile— you zap that one word, put in another word, and presto! But if you have to retype that entire poem on a typewriter to change one word, you hear the poem again in your head as you retype it. To even change one word I retype the whole poem. The rhythms become more familiar to me, I internalize what the poem sounds like, and then I'll come across other words that strike me as wrong—the break in this line doesn't have the right tension, let's say. Sometimes on the fiftieth typing, when I've got it memorized and my fingers are flying and I think I've combed out all the problems, I hear a false note, or something suddenly sounds flat. Yes, typing the poem over and over is really crucial to me.

With your editorial work at The New Yorker, *when do you find time to do your own writing?*

Right now, I'm not writing much. I have a new baby. Before, I could stay late at the office, or if we were at the beach I would take my little portable typewriter with me, but now I'm so engaged with the baby I've taken a break from writing. But ideas come and, even if I don't write for ten months, all that's happening up here in my mind will come back around if I work at it.

Poetry is not like lunch or like this conversation, where you set an appointment to get together at 11:30 and it happens. Mark Doty and I were talking yesterday about the life of the poet. He said that for years he functioned on inspiration—where for weeks or maybe months you don't write anything and sometimes in the middle of the night, lightning strikes, you have an idea, you get excited, you get up and go to the desk or the typewriter and set it down. But Mark said that as he's become older, he can't always wait for that. Life gets more complicated. Children. Professional commitments. You may not be lucky enough to have lightning strike every few months. You might have to say, Okay, I'm going to sit down at my typewriter and *court* inspiration.

Much of your inspiration comes from marriage. You and Galway Kinnell are alike in that.

I love marriage as a subject because it has to do with a running conversation between people. The domestic realm is so rich in contradictions—you live with another person and know them so well, yet you remain separate individuals. It's an infinitely strange thing that's hard to talk about. It's easier said in poetry— in images. In one of my poems there's the moment where a husband asks his wife to take off her dress. The mystery of that—the slight shock—between two people who know each other so well. It shouldn't be such a big deal, since we live together. But there is something wonderful about a man saying to his wife, "Take off your dress." And I tried to describe the moment when the arms cross, making the X, and she's both appearing and disappearing behind the fabric at the same time, as the dress comes off.

That image describes for me something between those two people that I would find hard to describe if you asked me to explain the mystery of desire in marriage. But a poem says much more than I could say to you in the abstract.

Reading your collection from start to finish, I'm struck by how the poems develop the story of a girl coming to woman-

hood. And the death of your father is one of the pivotal moments of passage.

It was the narrative event of my life in a way. I had a very nice middle-class existence. Grew up, went to school, then college. My father's death was the only thing I could say actually happened to me. It was a very double-edged event. In one way, it was the greatest sorrow of my life. I was fourteen and my father was so important to me. His death was devastating. But the flip side was that it very much defined who I am. There was an exhilaration when I realized I'd survived it, I could handle it, and I was going to go on and do a lot of things that he wouldn't be there to see. I felt a real kinship with other classmates who had lost a parent. I remember thinking, They're in that really tough club, the Dead Parent Club, and it was a quiet, silent club. We would never actually talk about it, but there is something about coming out on the other side of loss that has been very, very good for me. I don't know what to say.

Well, you say it in one poem.

You mean "Father, R.I.P., Sums Me Up at Twenty-Three." I'm a young woman there, and I'm imagining him critiquing me from beyond. And I hear his voice saying, "She has no head for politics, she craves good jewelry"—little things he might say are my flaws. And the poem is of course a self-criticism. When someone passes away and you internalize that voice, it's a way of keeping them with you; the voice that was his becomes a part of myself, and it comes through from time to time in my poetry.

Father, R.I.P., Sums Me Up at Twenty-Three

She has no head for politics,
craves good jewelry, trusts too readily,

marries too early. Then
one by one she sends away her friends

and stands apart, smug sapphire,
her answer to everything a slender

zero, a silent shrug—and every day
still hears me say she'll never be pretty.

Instead she reads novels, instead her belt
matches her shoes. She is master

of the condolence letter, and knows
how to please a man with her mouth:

Good. Nose too large, eyes too closely set,
hair not glorious blonde, not her mother's red,

nor the glossy black her younger sister has,
the little raven I loved best.

The conversation goes on.

Yes. That's absolutely right. The conversation goes on.

JANE HIRSHFIELD

*S*HE IS DEFINITELY *of this world. That's a flesh-and-blood woman at the microphone, speaking of "the ordinary hours, this ordinary earth." And yet the effect of her words is otherworldly, like the sound of far echoes in a canyon. The audience is spellbound, as if some visitation had taken their breath away. A few people begin to clap, awkwardly, the way a congregation will do when the choir is inspired and the moment transfigured and you want to applaud although applause seems too meager a salute to the sacred. The scatteredness of the clapping in this tent is unnerving; people stir, wanting to respond approvingly but uncertain how to do so. Gently, she puts us at ease: "In a large and generous audience like this," she says, "what I ask may not be possible, but I know that many of my poems don't evoke clapping, and I*

want to assure you that I take silence as a high compliment. If you could find in yourselves a way not to clap at all until the end, I would deeply appreciate that. We could try it. Maybe I shouldn't ask this, because if one person fails, or a few people, I know that will make everyone feel uncomfortable—but let's at least try."

And we do. She finishes the next poem to silence, the silence of deep contemplation. Once she said that a good poem can set its listener adrift in a small raft under a vast night sky of stars; at this moment we are drifting. She has written that we "travel by poem," as by any other means, so that we might see for ourselves more than would otherwise be seen. For Jane Hirshfield, poems are diaries of the journey. When we read them, "One person's word-wakened knowledge becomes another's."

It happened this night. The poet gathered her listeners into an intense Zen presence, into this moment's particular now—"the richest place to be."

Are you aware, at the end of a reading, of how the audience has been affected? Applause is only part of it.

When I read my work in public, mostly what I do is reinhabit the poem—its words, its feelings. I reenter the place where it originally unfolded within me in order to speak it back into the world again. But, of course, you can't help but also feel at some intuitive level how those words are being heard; a reading is actually very intimate in that way. Sometimes, at a reading's close, there is a great stillness. At first, that startled me, but I've learned to recognize that such a silence emerges when the audience has come to some deeply interior experience—and that is what I wish for myself when I hear or read a good poem.

Do you anticipate this kind of response when you are writing a poem?

Yeats once said that rhetoric is the argument you have with others, poetry is the argument you have with yourself. It's a wonderfully perceptive notion, because if you weren't arguing with yourself—figuring something out for yourself or working through some issue that's pressing itself upon your life—you could probably rest quite happily in silence. But because there is a fertile dilemma, a rich imbalance somewhere in your life or heart or understanding, you write a poem. I turn to poetry in order to address some flood or some gap, to stitch across a place of puzzlement or overspill or bewilderment or sorrow. When you first take a poem public, though, there's no way to know how the listener will react—all you can do is make it as meaningful, beautiful, and variegated for yourself as you can.

So you must know, before you start writing, what that fertile dilemma is—that puzzlement or bewilderment you need to address.

It depends. There are poems which come so clearly and immediately out of my experience that yes, I do know. Some large thing happens in my life, and a poem, for me, is the only possible response. But many other times, I don't really know what it is I am pondering at some deep level until I sit down to write. The poem is then the gate, as well as the field behind the gate. I discover my questions by entering my questions.

As you talk, I have this image in my head of you sitting in a quiet room, in the stark light of a lamp, writing. That image comes right out of "The Poet."

The Poet

She is working now, in a room
not unlike this one,
the one where I write, or you read.
Her table is covered with paper.
The light of the lamp would be
tempered by a shade, where the bulb's
single harshness might dissolve,
but it is not, she has taken it off.

Her poems? I will never know them,
though they are the ones I most need.
Even the alphabet she writes in
I cannot decipher. Her chair—
Let us imagine whether it is leather
or canvas, vinyl or wicker. Let her
have a chair, her shadeless lamp,
the table. Let one or two she loves
be in the next room. Let the door
be closed, the sleeping ones healthy.
Let her have time, and silence,
enough paper to make mistakes and go on.

Could you say something about how that poem came to be written, and about that shadeless lamp?

When I wrote "The Poet," I was a fellow at the Rockefeller Foundation's Center for Scholars and Artists in Bellagio, Italy. It's an extraordinary place, a centuries-old villa overlooking Lake Como, where extraordinary care is taken of you. I couldn't help but be aware of all the writers who will never have such good fortune—writers who may not have access to paper or ink or a bright enough lightbulb, writers for whom a quiet moment in which to work has to be stolen from the day. That person may write without the possibility of publication, or in a language not much translated, yet it matters immensely to me, and to us all, that her (or his) words and singular genius come into existence. That is one source-level of the poem. But there's another level as well, in which the figure in "The Poet" is something like my imagination of the Muse herself, working under every circumstance, in every place, and always in the service of increased light. She will do whatever she needs to do to magnify and clarify our experience of the world. That portrait of gift and determination lies also under the poem.

When did you first start wanting for yourself the time and silence that poem speaks of? When did you start writing?

I took to writing as soon as I was taught to write, in first or second grade. I wrote all through my childhood, secretly, in the middle of the night, hiding the evidence under my mattress. The written page was the field in which I developed the self that I became. I have no recollection of how it started—probably my first teacher, Mrs. Barlow, made one kind remark, and that was all it took: I was set on my course for life.

You're not the first poet to tell me she started writing early and wrote secretly and hid the poems away, in the closet or under the mattress.

Poetry is such a private and intimate exploration of self and world, at least for a person like me. There are writers who are natural extroverts. I imagine that extroverts write in an outward direction, to speak to somebody else. Introverts are different—we write to talk to ourselves, to find out who and what we are. How can you do that if you feel exposed, if you feel like you're performing? It's quite strange to me, even now, that my poems begin in utter solitude and privacy and yet I can somehow end up saying them, as I did here last night, in front of two thousand people. That's a difficult transition for a lot of introverted poets to make, and it was for me. And yet you do it, because you're so grateful that other people did. I owe so much to the poems of other poets, and to having heard other poets reading their work when I was young. They showed me the path to a viable life, a knowable life. When the world began to ask me to reciprocate, how could I say no?

I'm glad you're willing to read aloud—to perform, as it were. When it comes to poetry, some people are good readers and some people are good listeners. I have to confess that a poem often comes alive for me only when I hear it read—and by the poet herself.

It's a marvelous gift if you can hear the voice of the actual author, but then what do we do about works from the past? When you love poetry for a while, I think you come to develop an inner voice which is somehow chameleonlike, able to offer itself to whatever it encounters. You learn to listen to the musical scoring which inhabits the words, to the hints about tone which occur at the line breaks and in the punctuation. You can also say the poem aloud to yourself, and hear it that way. When you memorize poems by other people and put them through your own body and voice, the very musculature of the person who wrote the poem enters your body. Your mouth moves the way that person's mouth moved when he or she first "said" the poem by writing it—and that's true whether the poet spoke it or wrote the words in silence. The throat and larynx and breath are always moving a little when words travel through us.

What do you hope happens when you read in public?

That's an interesting question. Mostly I try not to hope at all. I try simply to be with the poem, to be in the poem. If I were more conscious of all the people in the audience, I would doubtless fall utterly silent. But if you are asking me what in the long run do I hope for when I give a poem to other people, it is that they might find in whatever caused me to articulate those particular words, feelings, thoughts, ideas, rhythms, something that also touches and changes them. I do think that a good poem alters you. How remarkable, if someone is touched by a poem of mine, if they too are altered and changed.

For that to happen, the poet first has to find her own true voice. I'm curious as to how you found yours.

My path was an odd, indirect one: I fell silent. I was a full-time student of Zen for eight years during my twenties, three of them in a monastery. During those three years I didn't write at all. But I learned how to pay attention, and I learned how to inhabit my own being a little more fully, and how to live in greater companionship with the rest of existence, both human and other-than-human. I don't think I would have managed to do that if I'd just gone on in the usual way. If you're not familiar with Zen, this probably sounds exotic, though Zen practice is really the opposite of exotic—and obviously I don't think every aspiring writer needs to follow such a path. Sometimes I think only a really slow learner like me needs to sit down for three years of silence in a Zen monastery before she can write.

What led you to the monastery?

I had read a number of Japanese and Chinese poems that communicated the essential feeling of Zen, and those images and ideas caught me. I was twenty-one when I began to study Zen—it was what I did instead of going to graduate school. You could say that intuition took me there, along with the usual measure of suffering. How does anyone decide their life course? You follow something you don't yet know but begin to feel is the right way for you. You dip in one finger. I went to look, and what I saw seemed like a good way for human beings to live. I also liked that in the Zen tradition, monastic practice is generally viewed as a limited period of intensive training, especially for a layperson. You're supposed to return to normal life, to a life that looks like everybody else's. But you return having learned how to pay attention, how to concentrate, and how to enter the experiences that concentration brings. You learn a little more about your relationship to the rest of existence—that your self is not quite what you thought it was, that in fact you are completely connected to all of life.

This is hard to talk about because the language of Zen is so interior. We don't yet have a spiritual vocabulary to talk about it publicly—certainly not in the West.

Mostly, of course, you don't explain Zen, you experience it. And so it's not surprising that, whether in the East or the West, you have to rely on metaphors to do the work of telling about that experience. Take, for example, one traditional image for awakened being, "snow in a silver bowl." Try to imagine, where does the snow end and the bowl begin? You can't quite tell, and so a sense of both containment and vastness inhabits that image. There's a whole constellation of such phrases, all of them like fingers pointing at the moon. In that way, the language of Zen isn't that different from the language of poetry.

Lyric poetry, as I see it, is fundamentally metaphorical in nature. For instance, in a poem in which a fence appears, the mind of the writer and the mind of the reader each inhabit "fence life," so to speak, for the moment that word appears in the poem. We enter into a much broader existence when we experience the stones and the weather, the material objects and the ongoing life around us, as a part of ourselves. The same is true, of course, for ideas, which can graze inside us like animals who reshape the landscape with their grazing. Poetry moves the mind and heart through so many different realms, so swiftly, so unnoticeably, that you can be carried by that current into a widened existence. The utter permeability of our life is made visible by the very nature of poetry.

What can you say about your own experience of Zen—I mean, insofar as it influences your writing?

The specific meditation practice is one of developing attentiveness to this moment, at first by settling your awareness within the breath while keeping your body centered and alert. You aren't doing anything but offering up your attention, yet somehow that "doing nothing" allows mind, body, emotion, the rain on the roof, to come together and reveal themselves. It's as if you were to sit very quietly in the woods: after a while, the animals begin to emerge, and you see the full amplitude of life that is in fact already there. The intention is to live your whole life in that kind of awareness. To be translucently awake—which should be simple, but somehow is quite hard—instead of living in a haze of distraction, hope, and fear, as we usually do. And you don't want to come to this state only in meditation: you want to be awake when you sand a floor or speak in a meeting or tie up the newspapers for recycling.

I try to be awake when I write a poem, and I think that Zen training showed me a way to do that. The combination of focused awareness and open permeability that goes into writing poetry is very similar to meditative mind, but the difference is that when I write, I am leaning my attention and my intention a little more into the realm of language, thought, and expression. Zen pretty much comes down to three things—everything changes; everything is connected; pay attention. It is simply a path toward entering your life more fully, a way of knowing the taste of your tongue in your own mouth. The path of poetry and shaped words is much the same, I think—each increases what we can know of human experience.

Isn't this connected to the Buddhist notion of mindfulness?

Yes, very deeply—mindfulness is the way that we open ourselves to both the inner and the outer worlds. Mindfulness, for instance, means that even as we're talking, I'm not only aware of what's going on between us—between our minds, our bodies, the air and space between us—but also aware of the fact that several people are attending to our conversation just now, quietly and politely on the periphery, and of the sound of the airplane that's passing overhead. Mindfulness recognizes that all this is part of what you and I say to each other. Even the person who ground the lenses in your glasses is participating in this conversation. And the driver of those trucks on the highway over there, and the carpenter who made the picnic table we're sitting on. In a state of open mindfulness, a broad subliminal attention is going out in many directions at once. Now, when you write a poem you are doing this all the time, sending out the tendrils of your attention, but you're also selecting which one of those directions is the most fertile and meaningful, which might add the most to the poem's communication and experience. Did that mosquito I just brushed away help or hinder our conversation? We didn't expect that mosquito to show up, or to talk about it once it did. If I were writing a poem, some part of me would be thinking, Do I let the mosquito in, or thank it and allow it to go on its way?

So much of your poetry strikes me as a meditation on mindfulness. For example, in a poem I especially like, you challenge us to look around and see.

That's an early poem, from 1982. I'm never sure whether I should call it a love poem or an end-of-love poem, because it is both those things.

For What Binds Us

There are names for what binds us:
strong forces, weak forces.
Look around, you can see them:
the skin that forms in a half-empty cup,
nails rusting into the places they join,
joints dovetailed on their own weight.
The way things stay so solidly
wherever they've been set down—
and gravity, scientists say, is weak.

And see how the flesh grows back
across a wound, with a great vehemence,
more strong
than the simple, untested surface before.
There's a name for it on horses,
when it comes back darker and raised: proud flesh,

as all flesh
is proud of its wounds, wears them
as honors given out after battle,
small triumphs pinned to the chest—

And when two people have loved each other
see how it is like a
scar between their bodies,
stronger, darker, and proud;
how the black cord makes of them a single fabric
that nothing can tear or mend.

Love as a "scar between their bodies" is a very powerful image. It's something I would never have contemplated except for a poet's imaginative use of language. That raises a question. I first knew your work as a translator—bringing us the poetry of others. Someone gave me a copy of your anthology Women in Praise of the Sacred, *with its scores of poems by women across the centuries. What gives you more pleasure, creating your own poetry—your own images—or translating the works of others?*

If I had to choose, it would be my own work—but when you're truly engaged in translation, the great joy is that it feels precisely like writing. The inspiration has been given you in the original text, but that magic act— that out of silence, language somehow begins to arise— provides the same thrill. Paul Valéry wrote that when he was translating the *Aeneid*, he'd occasionally find himself saying, "Well, it might have been better like this . . . ," as if he could revise Virgil. That thought occurs because, in the translating, the poem has come to feel as if it were the translator's own. Ethically, of course, a translator has to draw back from that temptation. But the experience of translating is as heady as being in love—the excitement, the anticipation, the joy of meeting and joining with the unknown.

Do you remember the turning point—how it happened that you fell in love with other women's poems?

In college, I had read a handful of poems by the two great Japanese women poets Ono no Komachi and Izumi Shikibu, who lived some thousand years ago. I read their poems and I saw in them my own life, and wanted to read more. I waited fifteen years for someone else to do that translation before taking it up myself, with a Japanese co-translator, Mariko Aratani, for what became the book *The Ink Dark Moon*. The truths and beauties of these poems are absolutely human truths and beauties. Their words were arrows that went directly to my heart, to its various hungers and turmoil. The fact that they came from an entirely different culture was a great confirmation for me of our basic human commonality, and of the ability of art to allow essential truths to cross great differences of time, culture, and language and still manage to speak as intimately as someone whispering into your ear in your own bed.

What kind of truth were those poems speaking?

In this case, the two great subject matters were erotic love and Buddhist awakening—two things which, as an eighteen-year-old, mattered a great deal to me. As they still do.

A good poem takes something you probably already know as a human being and somehow raises your capacity to feel it to a higher degree. It allows you to know your experience more intensely. When you meet your life in a great poem, it becomes expanded, extended, clarified, magnified, deepened in color, deepened in feeling. That path of knowledge started for me the day I bought my first book of poetry, when I was nine years old, for a dollar. It was a collection of Japanese haiku. I didn't really understand it, but I felt warmed as I read it, felt myself expanding, as if I were growing a larger set of roots. Whether from reading the New England Transcendentalists or Eskimo poetry, I feel that everything I know about being human has been deepened by the poems I've read. They've taught me how to be a human being.

And being human, for you, clearly includes a spiritual dimension. Many of the poems you have translated fall into that realm.

Yes, though I rather dislike that word, even when I find myself forced to use it. The abstract labels for what we call "spiritual" are all too narrow—they can't catch it, they're diminishing terms. If you turn instead to image or metaphor, the world begins to awaken. Here's an example of an awakening image, a poem Izumi Shikibu wrote that made a huge difference in my life.

> Although the wind
> blows terribly here,
> the moonlight also leaks

between the roofplanks
of this ruined house.

Now, moonlight is a traditional symbol for Buddhist enlightenment. But even if you don't know that, even if you understand the poem simply through the imagery of "weather," what it tells you is this: If your house is walled too tightly, if your psyche is so defended that it won't let in the cold winds—won't let in suffering or anger, won't let in grief—neither will it allow entrance to the desirable, beautiful moonlight. If you don't allow yourself to experience the full spectrum of human life, you won't wall out only the hard parts, you'll close yourself off from the luminous as well.

That poem taught me to be grateful to my difficulties. It has affected every day of my life since I translated it. Yet when I first worked on it, it was hard to understand: the words were there, but I didn't know what they meant. When finally the meaning fell into place, it was as if I had become that house and the moonlight had suddenly entered, changing everything.

I see a comparison between Shikibu's poem and your own "Letting What Enters Enter." Both speak to opening oneself to the unexpected, to life's opposites.

Letting What Enters Enter

Even in January rains
the blossoms open—
absence and longing
are also the plum-fragrant spring.
As the woman with her
sign and cart of rags is spring,
beside the highway, stepping slowly
through the undimmed flower of her life.
"What I now most want to happen
in my raving heart, make it happen—"
Sappho's cry to the goddess.
Who knows if that prayer was answered?
Each part holds the rest in the chill
spring rain and the silence; let one animal
eat from your hand and the whole herd comes.
But the woman was not beautiful
or whole in her own heart's raving,
and she forgave me nothing that I love.

That poem arose directly out of seeing a homeless
woman by the side of the highway over a period of
weeks. It was an early spring that year, and she was
always there, exactly as I describe her in the poem.
One day I thought, How can this woman not be

included in the spring's beauty? Just as the blossoms have room for the rain, so the spring has to have room for her. But in the end I judge myself through her eyes for that thought. I had brought this woman into my poem and talked about her as being as fully a part of spring in California as the January blossoms and rains. Then, belatedly remembering her reality, I realized the ethical problem: I may see her life as an undimmed flower, I may say that, but she may not experience it that way at all. She could, of course . . . but more likely not. And so it came to the last line: She does not forgive me for putting her in my poem. Nor should she.

We journalists can also feel a guilt over using people's stories and leaving their lives unchanged, but I think your including her is a tribute to the dignity of a life despite misfortune and adversity, and I find it so helpful to see how an image from your ordinary, daily experience comes to inhabit a poem. What about the images in "Mule Heart"?

That is one of a group of poems in *The Lives of the Heart* which I think of as a series of recipes for getting through difficult periods, times you feel you've walked over a cliff, times Winston Churchill referred to as "visits of the black dog." There are a number of different prescriptions throughout the book. The strategy of the mule's heart is sheer stubbornness: grit your teeth and get through it.

The poem begins with reference to "two waiting baskets."
Tell me how those baskets became part of the poem.

I was in Greece many years ago and saw how they put pannier baskets on the sides of the mules to carry things up and down the steep coastline. In the poem, the basket placed on one side of the stubborn heart is filled with all the things you would want to keep: the fragrant lemons, the things you love. The other basket is for holding your griefs, your sorrows, everything that has abandoned you—which of course by the end of our lives will be everything, including our lives themselves. Each of these aspects of life the mule heart must carry: it carries our joys, and it carries our sufferings. Maybe the two baskets mean that they balance, somehow.

Many years passed between my seeing the little mules of Santorini and writing the poem. I wrote it to help me get through a time in my life when I thought a certain stubbornness would help. I told myself, "Just last out the moment, and rely on the truth that everything changes; if you can simply hang in there, you'll be all right." And from that feeling, the poem came. A

wonderful thing about poetry is that at any moment a
poem draws on everything you have ever known, seen,
experienced. A poem is like those baskets, needing to be
filled, and so your whole life must be available to each
poem as you write it. This poem needed those mules,
their flies and braided, belled bridles. Sometimes I
think that poems use us in order to think, to do their
own work. You know, most of the time I feel as if I am
in the service of the poem—a poem isn't something I
make, it's something I serve.

Mule Heart

On the days when the rest
have failed you,
let this much be yours—
flies, dust, an unnameable odor,
the two waiting baskets:
one for the lemons and passion,
the other for all you have lost.
Both empty,
it will come to your shoulder,
breathe slowly against your bare arm.
If you offer it hay, it will eat.
Offered nothing,
it will stand as long as you ask.
The little bells of the bridle will hang

beside you quietly,
in the heat and the tree's thin shade.
Do not let its sparse mane deceive you,
or the way the left ear swivels into dream.
This too is a gift of the gods,
calm and complete.

I've read that the path you've chosen for yourself is what the Japanese call teahouse practice. What does that mean?

I think we may have just burned down my teahouse with this conversation. Teahouse practice means that you don't explicitly talk about Zen. It refers to leading your life as if you were an old woman who has a teahouse by the side of the road. Nobody knows why they like to go there, they just feel good drinking her tea. She's not known as a Buddhist teacher, she doesn't say, "This is the Zen teahouse." All she does is simply serve tea—but still, her decades of attentiveness are part of the way she does it. No one knows about her faithful attention to the practice, it's just there, in the serving of the tea and the way she cleans the counters and washes the cups.

That is the practice-path I've felt was right for my poems. Though the facts of my life seem to have become known over the years, there are almost no explicit references to Zen in my poetry—fewer than you can find in many poets who have never done any kind of formal Buddhist training. And still, people seem to recognize that something is there. So that's the state of my "teahouse practice" these days. When I talk about Zen, as I have here with you, my teahouse has a pretty leaky roof—but maybe my poems can continue following that path, just keep wiping down the counter and pouring hot water over fragrant leaves.

KURTIS LAMKIN

A SEA OF *hands rises in the tent, swelling and falling like waves. Ripple follows ripple across the cavernous space, moving as if directed by a single will. On stage Kurtis Lamkin plucks the strings of an instrument I had seen once before, on my first visit to West Africa almost forty years ago. The kora is a branch of the harp family. Twenty-one strings run perpendicular, arching like the wires of a suspension bridge along a neck that extends three feet from a large resonating gourd pressed against the poet's thighs. The sounds from Lamkin's fingers flying up and down the strings give his words wings to rise. His eyes close. Sweat trickles down his temples. His words dissolve into a rhythmic cadence that encircles the audience with a hoop of swaying syllables:* di di dee yoo doe di di dee yooo do dedo oh. *Now his voice grows barely audible, the*

fingers slow in flight, the music dies away. The upraised hands gradually cease their motion, and the tent grows still and quiet like the sea at rest.

Your playing and reciting remind me of that deep interior connection between music and poetry—and their capacity to stir the listener's soul. When did you know that the kora and poetry were meant for each other?

About fifteen years ago I was living in New York and Papa Suso was performing on the kora at the Brooklyn Museum. Papa Suso is an internationally renowned djeli—a poet-troubadour. Along with other master djelis—Foday Musa Suso and Salieu Suso—he is a member of the Suso clan, which over many generations has been known for its excellence in kora playing and recitation. When I heard the sound I almost swooned. This instrument talks. The kora talks. I knew it would be perfect for poetry. It's like the human voice, speaking—and speaking with a range of sounds that connect the words a person is saying to the deepest reaches of the inner, emotional life. When I'm touching these strings, I'm touching a lifeline inside the listener.

Then I went to West Africa, where the kora is as common as a guitar. And I met djelis who use the kora along with other traditional instruments. The sound was coming not only from deep inside them but from somewhere in the far past as well. In the oral tradition they pass on from one generation to another the tales and prayers and poems of the past. I even heard of djelis who would be called into court to testify to how a boundary had been set many, many years ago; there was no written record, but the description became part of the remembered tale and was accepted in court because it was so reliable. So the kora is used to talk about people's lives, the kind of society they've agreed on, and to conjure up new stories.

Do you compose stories as you play?

Definitely, definitely. I often play the kora in the middle of the night because—well, basically I dream out loud with it. There are times when I can feel the charge going back and forth between me and the kora. It's like a dance. The voice of the kora and my voice going back and forth. I live in Charleston, South Carolina, and sometimes I take the kora down to the beach, to the ocean. I hold it up and can hear the wind blowing through the strings. It sounds like a choir. And it feeds me, it feeds me. I want to put into words my response to the music.

When you wake up during the night, have you been dreaming?

Yes, and the poem may be part of the dream. But it's difficult for me to wake up and try to capture the dream, so what I like to do is to compose a poem that invites it back. Little by little the dream returns.

Do you write it down?

Not anymore. I compose by heart in the oral tradition, speaking it over and over and over, savoring it, revising it, until it starts to take a shape of its own. It comes alive, and it lives in my head as clearly as if I had written down the letters on a page. Whether you are writing with the kora, or without the kora, on the page or on a computer, you still have to come to that source inside you where the vision is—those impressions that you collect through your life are registered indelibly on your soul. Some people go to that source when they make words on the page; I do it when the strings of the kora and my imagination are dancing together.

So not all your poems arise in dreams.

Oh, no. I'd say most come from firsthand encounters. A lot of what I do comes right off the street, from encounters in everyday life. Like my poem "jump mama." I was on 125th Street in Harlem one day—lots of people out on the street—and I saw this woman walking down the street, passing by all those vendors, and when she got near, I realized that woman was my wife. Actually my wife. And the next time I picked up the kora, this poem started emerging.

jump mama

pretty summer day
grammama sittin on her porch
easy
rockin her grandbaby in her wide lap
ol men sittin in their lincoln
tastin and talkin and talkin and tastin
young boys on the corner
milkin a yak yak   wild hands   baggy pants
young girls halfway up the block
jumpin that double dutch
singin their song
kenny kana paula
be on time
cause school begins
at a quarter to nine
jump one two three and aaaaaaah . . .

round the corner comes
this young woman

draggin herself heavy home from work
she sees the young boys
sees the old men
but when she sees the girls she just starts smilin
she says let me get a little bit of that
they say   you can't jump
you too old

why they say that
o, why they say that

she says tanya you hold my work bag
chaniqua come over here girl i want you to hold my handbag
josie could you hold my grocery bag
please
kebè take my purse
she starts bobbin her head, jackin her arms
tryin to catch the rhythm of the ropes
and when she jumps inside those turning loops
the girls crowd her   sing their song
kenny kana paula
be on time
cause school begins
at a quarter to nine
jump one two three and
aaaaaaaaaaaaaaaaaaaaaaaaaaaaah
she jumps on one leg—*aaaaah*

she dances sassy   saucy—*aaaaah*
jump for the girls mama
jump for the stars mama
jump for the young boys sayin
jump mama!   jump mama!
jump for the old woman sayin—aww, go head baby

and what the young girls say
what the young girls say
aaaaaaaaaaaaaaaaaaaaaaaaaaaaaaaaaaaaaaaah

You were introduced here at the festival as a poet who explores the terrain between the fixed meanings of words and the raw sounds produced by "scatting." I didn't know what scatting was until I heard the long, drawn out aaaaaaaaaah *in that poem.*

Scatting means dissolving words into sounds. It's a kind of jazz singing in which you improvise as you go and then sing to a melody. You say the words in such a way that you cannot identify the meaning of the sound but it still has the quality or feeling a word might evoke. You can drag it out slowly or faster according to the texture of the sound, not the definition of the word. It's a marvelous way of articulating what is in your soul through the music of the sound. Now, when I'm playing, the rhythms and melodies of the strings and the ideas in my head start making their own poetry in a kind of point-counterpoint. If I were to write each poem down —which I rarely do—you'd see it has a firm structure and can be recalled word for word. But when I perform the poems I am always open to new relationships between the music and the lyrics. Sometimes I think that when I am composing I deal with everything in 3-D—that in composing or performing it's like I am breathing on the things in the poem, and they respond by turning the breath into words.

Well, however it happens, the result is effective as performance poetry. The audience was breathing along with you, if that's the way to put it. They were caught up in the experience.

That's the beautiful thing about being here at this festival. They call it a festival, but it's like a carnival—and you're the ride! It's really interesting. One person in the audience may be thinking about where he parked the car and how he's going to get out after the event. Someone else may be thinking about that appointment she has with the dentist tomorrow. But sooner or later you feel their minds and yours are one, and suddenly everyone's involved. Performing poems is really about the mind and how it can be visited by people all at once through language.

That happened here when you performed "those crazy beach girls."

That response was wonderful, wasn't it? I do a lot of my composing while I am strolling on the beach, playing the kora. Sometimes I fall into a rhythm where it looks like the ocean is dancing to my tune. It's powerful even to entertain the notion that you can have an effect on something as awesome as the ocean! Now, that happens sometimes with an audience. When I got to that poem last night, the audience was ready. We were in sync. I looked out and they were waving their hands like the waves of the ocean. I'd never experienced something quite like that before.

those crazy beach girls

those crazy beach girls take you to the sea
and then they act like monsters
from the deep
they wanna scare you—support them
shake something

and when you creep back to the beach at night
silk the light   silk the moon   silk the light on tide
just let it haunt
that girltalk
shake something   shake something

if you shake your head you shake the moonrise
if you shake your arms
the wind will embrace you
surprised you take two steps back
the sea will take two steps up
and when you take two steps the sea moves
easy
easy on you
the seacrests pop in the nightblue
the stars spinning in their sockets   and the dunes
ripples beneath your feet
take   your   time
shake   your   soul
shake your heiny shake a heaven
shake your heiny shake a heaven
shake your heiny your heaven your heaven heiny shake

those crazy beach girls take you to the sea
shake the girls shake the world shake the tide shake the pier
shake something   shake something

*It's a long way from that beach to the Million Man March
in Washington. You wrote a poem about that experience, too.*

Yes, I went to that march because I wanted to
affirm, or confirm, that there are as many different
kinds of black men as there are black men. I wanted to

see us all together. What happened was more than I had anticipated. There were so many, many of us, and we weren't alike in our dress, in our faith, in our beliefs. And everybody was there for very individual reasons. But the idea of being together was enough. That was enough. If nothing else ever happened, the idea of our being together was so valuable because we had been apart for so long—ever since we'd been taken from Africa and brought west. Now I saw men sitting on the steps, crying. I saw men resting on each other's shoulders. I saw strangers talking to each other as if they were old friends. And I'll tell you what was the most powerful experience. It was when we fell silent together. That a million people could be silent at once is hard to imagine. The silence took on a presence all its own. It was incomparable. As I'm looking around I start writing this poem. Line by line it was coming into place. By the time I got home it was there, inside me.

the million man march

we do right
we do wrong
we do time   overtime
we do what it takes to shake the snake

that coils around our humble lives
whatever we can do
we do

we do lunch
we do meetings
we do fundraisers   we do marches
we send a million men
to carry peace to the heart of a cold cold nation
some say we don't count
we do
we always do

suppose there's a god
who thinks that we are god
who loves us so deeply she followed us here
we work so hard every trick looks like a miracle
and then we name the trickster god
if there is a god
who thinks that we are god
do we hear her prayer
do we?

in the deep dark hour
when we are all alone

what is that sound   what is that prayer
what is this faith
we do

What's behind these words: "suppose there's a god / who thinks that we are god / who loves us so deeply she followed us here"?

I believe that just beyond all that I can understand there is a divine being upon whom I can call, a divinity that flows from an ultimate devotion beyond time, space, and understanding. Suppose this being believes that I, too, can be called upon. That such a possibility existed became clear to me after I went to West Africa, to an island off the coast of Senegal called Gorée. It was the last point in Africa from which many Africans were sent to the Western Hemisphere and slavery. The doorway through which they marched across a plank onto the slaver's ship was called the "Door of No Return" because once you went through that door you were never, ever expected to come back. My ancestors must have passed there, and now I had returned to the Door of No Return. Days later the irony struck me with such a force that I cried—to realize that I am part of this story. Something took me back, to a place and time I did not know I had been before. Life is circular, it is winding—but how open are we to where it takes us?

We pray for that, and we hope our god is listening, that we're being heard. But what if our god is praying to us? What if our god is asking us for things? Are we listening? Are we open? Why would such thoughts come from the Door of No Return? That's the mystery.

I know it's not easy to make a living as a performance poet, but it seems to be a calling to you. Perhaps that is part of the mystery.

As I get older it keeps me fresh. It keeps me in the groove. The djelis of West Africa went out as troubadours in part because they wanted to learn what was happening in the world, and they wanted to incorporate it into their own experience. I feel the same way. Knowing that I can do this makes me get up in the morning with a clear hunger, a hunger to hold on to something that day that is rare and elusive. Once I saw a moon with a blue ring about it. I thought it looked like a doorway between me and the sky. I wanted to hold it, to possess it, but obviously I couldn't hold it or own it. But in the poem I can hold it, because it's become a part of me. The hunger is to hold on to what's miraculous.

When were you first exposed to music and poetry?

My mother would cook and sing spirituals around the

house—she's from South Carolina. And my father—he's from Georgia—would shave and hum blues. The strange thing is that I never heard my father sing lyrics, or more precisely, words. My mother did, but even though you could hear my father throughout the house all the time, you only heard sounds, not words. I got into composing by heart when I was a kid because when I couldn't sleep I would go into the living room, in the middle of the night, by myself, and I would rock in a chair, muttering what was on my mind. Sometimes I would stand up and talk or sing out loud. I have composed strictly by heart; I have written poems on the page; and I have composed poems with the kora. Each way has its own flow and feel, and the variations—the technical variations—of each are endless. But all of them have one thing in common, which is that words make things become, and these beings move, if not in the world around us then in the world within us.

So, when did you know you wanted to do this with your life?

By high school I was writing, and I came to New York in the late seventies wanting to become a writer. I was a short-order cook during the day, and at night I would stay in my apartment in Harlem and write. One day someone in the cafeteria where I was working introduced me to Claude Brown, whose *Manchild in the Promised Land* I had read. He was a hero to me. When I met him he took me outside and standing there was James Baldwin! Can you believe it? They both stood on the street singing the blues to me about how hard it was to become a writer, how you had to get used to rejections, meet all the deadlines, and still you might not make a living. They just about had me convinced that it was too hard when they told me to go for it. And they told me never to lose the inspiration to speak, to tell my stories.

Then there was an incident in St. Louis. During the day I would sit in the library reading Langston Hughes, and at night I went out looking for trouble. One day I was about to get on a bus to carry on down in Little Rock, and a policeman stopped me. The first time a policeman stopped me that summer! And he asked me what I had in my bag. I showed him the bag and he went through it. He found what I had been writing at the library. He said, "These are poems?" I said, "Yeah." He said, "You a poet?" I said, "Yeah." He threw them on the ground and cursed me. I guess he didn't like people like me writing poetry. And I said to myself, "Oh, God, oh God. On any other day he could have stopped me and found the shotgun I was carrying. Now he's only found poems—and still he's cursing me." He had a gun on his hip, and I knew where mine was. But it hit me: The guns didn't make either of us a better man. I came to my senses. I decided that if I'm going to die, then let me starve as a poet. I changed my ticket and went back to Philly and started writing. And that was it. A lot of things turned me around, of course. But if I could put my finger on the one thing that has sustained me, it would definitely be poetry. Yeah, poetry.

SHIRLEY GEOK-LIN LIM

I PUSH THE *pedal on the golf cart, and we lunge across the small bridge next to the sweet shop. My passenger squeezes the bag and books on her lap tightly and laughs. Pedestrians along the narrow road—some reading from poetry books—look up and wave. She waves back. It is hard to imagine her arriving in America in 1969, shabby, uprooted, and poor. She had fled the poverty of the Chinese minority in Malaysia and come to Boston to study at Brandeis University. Feeling an absence of place—"myself absent in America"—she searched for a new home and struggled to cope with the strangeness. The title of her memoir,* Among the White Moon Faces, *embodies her feelings of otherness. Here at the festival, however, she is assured and assuring as she reads her poems about those immigrant years, poems that*

helped her become the first woman and first Asian to win the Commonwealth Poetry Prize. Last night I scanned her eleven-page résumé, an all-American testament to the outsider's impatience, the gritty resolve to infiltrate the barricades and triumph from within. As an archetype from our immigrant history, the story is familiar, but every immigrant's life is coin freshly minted, and Shirley Geok-lin Lim has fashioned her own American story as wife, mother, teacher, and poet. It is poetry, she says, that helped the rebellious and restless nomad find herself and her place. "Listening and telling my own stories," she says, "I am moving home." In central New Jersey on a golf cart, no longer absent in America.

When you were reading "Pantoun for Chinese Women," I could have heard a pin drop. The young people were giving you their rapt attention.

If teenagers understand one thing, it's anger. The experience deals with childbirth and female infanticide. Many of those students listening were young women, and I suspect they could relate across cultures and histories to a society where women are less valued than males. That may have been a point of entry for them. But I did not write the poem to get an audience response, and when the audience responds it's always a surprise to me.

Why did you write it?

It has to do with my growing up in a traditional Chinese society—the ethnic Chinese community in Malaysia. I was a girl in a family of eight boys, so I was very precious to my father, which was rare, because in traditional Chinese societies, as you may know, girls are not valued. I grew up knowing that I was one of the fortunate who were wanted and loved. One day I read in *The New York Times* about the consequence of the one-child policy in China. China is a country with over a billion people. Its environment has been degraded completely by overpopulation. One of the horrible consequences of this one-child policy is female infanticide. Baby girls are put to death. When I read that, I was so outraged, so angry, that I wrote this poem. And to control my anger, I wrote it in the strictest form I could think of—a pantoun, which features a great deal of repetition. The pantoun has often been used for comic purposes because of the repetition and the structure. But I realized I could use the form to control my anger.

How is that? How does form help to control your emotions?

The pantoun requires a very disciplined focus; you can't allow things to spill over. You have to be very focused, like a laser that produces a powerful intensity. I have to do that with my emotions all the time when I write. I think that's what most writers do. They sit down and concentrate. It's as if you tap into your alpha waves. Otherwise, your mind is constantly wandering as the world calls out to it. That's ordinary, everyday consciousness. But I believe that the consciousness from which creativity comes is this intensity of focus that is the result of practice. Sylvia Plath wrote exercise poems. Writing poetry is itself a form of exercise, a discipline as much as it is a calling and an art. And a discipline always asks for exercise. I tell my students that you can't read about playing tennis in a book and then go out and be a good tennis player. You have to be out there hitting that ball and hitting it again and again to become the best tennis player possible. So if you want to be a good poet, you have to be working and working and working on the craft. Practice. Practice. Practice.

With that background, would you read it again for me now?

First let me just tell you that one of the favorite methods of killing these little baby girls is to turn their faces over in soot. Soot is readily available in peasant homes, and you don't have to reuse it. You can throw it out with the infant.

SHIRLEY GEOK-LIN LIM

Pantoun for Chinese Women

"At present, the phenomena of butchering, drowning
and leaving to die female infants have been very serious."
(*The People's Daily*, Peking, March 3rd, 1983)

They say a child with two mouths is no good.
In the slippery wet, a hollow space,
Smooth, gumming, echoing wide for food,
No wonder my man is not here at his place.

In the slippery wet, a hollow space,
A slit narrowly sheathed within its hood.
No wonder my man is not here at his place:
He is digging for the dragon jar of soot.

That slit narrowly sheathed within its hood!
His mother, squatting, coughs by the fire's blaze
While he digs for the dragon jar of soot.
We had saved for a hundred days.

His mother, squatting, coughs by the fire's blaze.
The child kicks against me mewing like a flute.
We had saved ashes for a hundred days.
Knowing, if the time came, that we would.

The child kicks against me crying like a flute
Through its two weak mouths. His mother prays
Knowing when the time comes that we would,
For broken clay is never set in glaze.

Through her two weak mouths his mother prays.
She will not pluck the rooster nor serve its blood,
For broken clay is never set in glaze:
Women are made of river sand and wood.

She will not pluck the rooster nor serve its blood.
My husband frowns, pretending in his haste
Women are made of river sand and wood.
Milk soaks the bedding. I cannot bear the waste.

My husband frowns, pretending in his haste.
Oh clean the girl, dress her in ashy soot!
Milk soaks our bedding, I cannot bear the waste.
They say a child with two mouths is no good.

You may have contained the anger, but not the sadness.

I hope it's clear that the anger is not against men.
The mother-in-law herself participates in the deed.
The anger is at an age-old structure that refuses to
change. I hope the poem is one more fist beating down
that wall.

I want to ask you about another poem you read earlier to the audience here. It's the one you call "Lament."

Yes. I grew up in a household in Malaysia that spoke Malay and Hokkein. I went to an English-language school and was educated by Irish nuns. Then I came to the United States at the age of twenty-four. I wrote this poem because in coming to the United States I was suffering the loss of my community. But determined as I was *not* to return to a country where I would face governmental barriers on account of my ethnicity, language choice, and gender, I was also aware that in the United States I was meeting prejudice because of my accent and Asian background. The lament is in some ways a praise song, a love poem to the English language, which, together with other languages like Spanish and Chinese, I continue to view as a wonderful achievement of the human species. The English language is capable of overcoming the separate identities that divide us even as it sometimes is deployed in erecting those separations.

Lament

I have been faithful
To you, my language,
Language of my dreams,

My sex, my laughter, my curses.
How often have I
Stumbled, catching you
Short when you should be
Free, snagging on curves,
Till fools have called me
Fool. How often have you
Betrayed me, faithless!
Disowned me—a woman
You could never marry,
Whom you have tired
Of long ago.

I have been faithful
Only to you,
My language. I choose you
Before country,
Before what eyes see,
Mouth, full-hearted, taste.
I choose you before
Lover and husband,
Yes, if need be,
Before child in arms,
Before history and all
It makes, belonging,
Rest in the soil,
Although everyone knows

You are not mine.
They wink knowingly
At my stupidity—
I, stranger, foreigner,
Claiming rights to
What I have no right—
Sacrifice, tongue
Broken by fear.

Your poems draw so deeply from the experience of family. You were abandoned by your mother—that certainly left its mark.

Well, in a Chinese family it's easier to think about being abandoned by fathers, right? Maybe it is in most families. But when a mother leaves home, you lose the pillar in your life, because you look to your mother for strength. I keep thinking of Nora in Ibsen's *A Doll's House*. She walks out of the house, bangs the door, and enters a new life. She feels she has the right to a new life. But I also say, "What about the children you leave behind? Nora, you can't walk through that door! You can't leave those kids behind you." Nora may have thought of herself as a feminist who believed she had a sacred duty to herself. We women do have sacred duties to ourselves, but we have a sacred duty to our children, too.

So you still question your mother's abandonment of you?

I think I will never accept it.

You've never seen her since then?

I have. I have. I met her again when I was sixteen. But then when I met her the second time, at the age of eighteen, she had found a new man. She wanted me to call her Auntie in front of this man. That was the second abandonment. I never forgave her for it.

And what about your father?

My father loved his children. He wanted every single one of us. This is the irony of the reversal, you know? Usually people think of mothers with children and not men, but we were the center of his life. He was also, unfortunately, a very violent man. He could not control his temper, and he beat us. Familial relationships are never simple, are they? I think if you had a simple family life, you would have been very lucky. Love is so complicated. My father loved us, but he beat us! How do you come to terms with this very loving man who also was an abusive man?

What did it do for you to grow up with eight brothers?

I think it made me very motivated not to be a girl. I wasn't going to cry. I wasn't going to be weak. I wasn't going to ask for help. I was going to be as independent as I could. In a way it's been very helpful, because women who grew up thinking that they were going to be nurtured by men, frequently they are really disappointed. There is no Prince Charming. And the sooner you learn that you have to be independent, that you are alone, and if there are people to help you it's a blessing, but it's not a given—I think this is the beginning of strength and wisdom.

I ask these questions because in your memoir you combine language and memory as the foundation for your poetry. It's obvious that writing about your family has helped to create a center of stability for your life and a center of gravity for your poetry.

Poetry is what has saved me through the years. I started writing when I was about nine. I discovered that I could go into a space where there is language— language that is mine, which is completely private and where I can do anything with it. I can curse at someone I cannot curse otherwise. I can create a space of beauty when all around me is poverty and deprivation. I can experience an uplifting of the spirit when all around me things are trying to pull me down. That act of writing the poem is the act that has centered me all my life.

You talk about beauty and uplifting the spirit, yet so many of your poems deal with pain and grief.

If we are to survive, isn't it important for us to get pleasure in some way, even in the deepest pain and grief? Isn't this how we keep from sinking and drowning? There's a poem by Stevie Smith with the title "Not Waving but Drowning." The poem tells of people along a shore watching a swimmer, and the swimmer is waving, and everyone is thinking, She's waving, we'll wave back. But the swimmer is really drowning. There's something to this notion in poetry. The poet is not waving, but drowning.

A new book of your poetry has just been published: What the Fortune Teller Didn't Say.

It's really a rather skinny book. When you think of it—that this is a book that came out of ten years of writing poetry—it sure isn't much.

Well, you've been teaching. When did you find the time to write?

I usually write when I get up at three or four in the morning. That's the little space I have. I might have to take early retirement to produce a bigger book.

What was it the fortune teller didn't say?

What the fortune teller didn't say was that I would come to the United States.

What the fortune teller didn't say

When the old man and his crow
picked the long folded parchment
to tell my fortune at five,
they never told about leaving,
the burning tarmac and giant wheels.
Or arriving—why immigrants
fear the malice of citizens
and dull shutterings of those
who hate you whatever you do.

My mother did not grip
my hand more possessively.
Did I cry and was it corn
ice-cream she fed me because
the bird foretold a husband?

Wedded to unhappiness,
she knew I would make it,
meaning money, a Mercedes
and men. She saw them shining

in the tropical mildew
that greened the corner alley
where the blind man and his
moulting crow squatted
promising my five-year-old hand
this future. Of large faith
she thrust a practical note
into the bamboo container,
a shiny brown cylinder
I wanted for myself, for
a cage for field crickets.

With this fortune my mother bought,
only the husband is present,
white as a peeled root, furry
with good intentions, his big nose
smelling a scam. Sometimes,
living with him, like that
black silent crow I shake
the cylinder of memory
and tell my fortune all over again.

My mother returns, bearing
the bamboo that we will fill
with green singing crickets.

*Hearing you read that poem, it seems to me you were des-
tined to become an American. Here you are, born in
Malaysia during the Japanese occupation, of an ethnic Chi-
nese background, having come to the United States and mar-
ried a Jewish American.*

I have a wonderful Jewish American boy who identi-
fies himself as an Asian American. His name is Gershom.

I mean, you had to become American with that life story.

You think so?

*Where else would you have gone to become the whole of
your parts?*

I think the rest of the world should be like that. The
rest of the world should be open to those kinds of
transformations. I don't think the rest of the world
should become American. That's not what I'm saying.
There's so much of this mixing occurring all over the
world, and the political stability and openness to the

transformations that are happening here are not in place yet. America allows it to happen, although not without pain.

In the workshop for students, you were asked by some of the young people to define yourself.

I tell them that, politically, I'm an American citizen, and I am damned proud of it. I'm very lucky to be an American citizen, because I'm protected by the Constitution. So, first thing I would say, I'm an American citizen. And secondly, I would say that in the deepest ways that move me, I am a mother.

My favorite poem in your collection is "Learning to love America."

This is the immigrant's experience. It's also a mother-son poem. It is a poem for my son.

Learning to love America

because it has no pure products

because the Pacific Ocean sweeps along the coastline
because the water of the ocean is cold
and because land is better than ocean

because I say we rather than they

because I live in California
I have eaten fresh artichokes
And jacarandas bloom in April and May

because my senses have caught up with my body
my breath with the air it swallows
my hunger with my mouth

because I walk barefoot in my house

because I have nursed my son at my breast
because he is a strong American boy
because I have seen his eyes redden when he is asked
    who he is
because he answers I don't know

because to have a son is to have a country
because my son will bury me here
because countries are in our blood and we bleed them

because it is late and too late to change my mind
because it is time.

*You've written that you became an American politically
with the birth of your son.*

Yes, before my son was born I was a displaced person, emotionally bound on one territory but receiving support from a different society and living the dissonant condition of the exile or refugee. When my son was born I became protective of his rights as an American; that is, I wanted the recognition of being a fellow American *for* my child because I did not want him to suffer from my history of displacement. The political and social struggle for civil rights itself can transform the outsider into a citizen.

Have you read that poem to your son?

I never show my poems to my son. I never show my poems to my husband. It's weird. I share my poems, I guess, with unknown people, and I don't share them with the people I'm most intimate with. It's like going to a bar. You know the old story about how people will go to a bar and they'll tell the bartender all kinds of things that they would never tell their wives or their husbands? There's a part of me that I would like to keep sheltered that comes out in language, and once it's out in language, it's shared with the rest of the world. But I want to shelter it from the people I spend my life with. I don't know if that makes any sense. But they know me in person. There's another me on the printed page.

It's paradoxical, I know. Poems are private utterances, and sharing them at a festival like this is exciting because people are receptive to poetry, but it's a strange mutation of the very privacy of the art which appears on the page and then gets transmuted into a public reading. I'm not sure I like it altogether.

Because?

Because I'm worried that if that's all poets think about— the public transmutation—then the basic primary first act of a private meditation will be lost. That's what I'm afraid of.

I don't think it's a concern in your case. Home and family seem forever a part of the poetry you compose.

They have to be. Home and place are where we humans are grounded. We don't live in motel rooms. God save us if we start living in motel rooms! That's the human experience. It's not just a woman's experience. Men who live alone find that they want to have a home, too. They start buying good furniture and nice plates. This desire runs very deep in our nature.

It's the need for intimacy, don't you think? Our yearning for it seems so much more powerful than our capacity to expe-

rience it. You hint at that in "Starry night," which is one of my favorites in your new book.

Starry night

He could always find Orion;
although young
he saw the innocent sword.

Because I was his mother
I could not speak what boys
should know. No sharing of manhood

between us. I keep silence
before the faintly moving stars.

I think of "Starry night" as a lyrical meditation on the relation between mother and son. The young boy may be innocent, that is, ignorant and naïve, but unlike his mother, he understands "manhood" as his existential condition. As a woman, the mother admits this mystery about her son; she admits the limitations of what she can know about him. Orion is the name of a large, brilliant constellation of stars, figured as a hunter with belt and hound, coming from the Greek mythological hunter Orion, who was killed by the god Artemis. The son's ability to recognize Orion suggests his innate acknowledgment of his male subjectivity. But the image of Orion, the hunter, is both powerful and tragic. Incipient manhood carries with it the possibilities of tragic development, not simply strength and power but also violence and death. The mother's silence is a kind of wisdom before what must remain a mystery to her, and what she recognizes as an inevitable separation as her son grows up.

Yet the poem is also silent about the mother's feelings.

It is. I wished to leave this evocative, unspoken space for the readers to fill up with their own emotions. Perhaps a father, a son, reading it will respond differently; and reading the poem under different conditions, the same reader might discover a different emotion in it—grief at separation, acceptance, joy in the mystery of the son's separate life, perhaps a moment of clarity at the illumination of a relationship.

Like most lyrical poems, this was a "spontaneous" utterance. I had been struck repeatedly by my son's stargazing skill. He was about ten then, prepuberty, and we were very close. I was raising him alone while my husband was teaching in Atlanta, three thousand miles away from Santa Barbara. The poem actually arrived a few years later, when he was in his teens and distancing himself from his mother. The image of the young boy recognizing Orion on the horizon must have been working in my imagination for a long while, and the poem came out pretty straight, an utterance of grief, and celebration, at his growing up. Despite its spontaneity, it did not come from a moment of pain. As I recall it, I had taken some time to devote to writing poetry, and the poem wrote itself.

What does that say about the creative process of poetry?

I suppose it is an example of the inexplicability of the creative process. It works through ordinary feelings, familiar relationships, even when it sets itself a grand or historical challenge. But it seizes on what is hidden from everyday view, the strangeness in our dailiness that we need to make meaning of or for. The creative process is uncanny. It remains unknowable because it works with the not yet known. As for the conditions that support creativity, I know what I need as a poet. I need time—quiet time—and pen and paper.

PAUL MULDOON

THE EMCEE INTRODUCES *him as one of Ireland's finest poets, and the moment Paul Muldoon starts reading, you hear echoes of his country's history in his voice. The puckish wit and furrowed melancholy sail side by side like ships of the same fleet. Muldoon's reputation for anecdote, invention, and parable—for skywriting acts with lyrics, sonnets, and ballads—precedes him to the festival. So does his penchant for pulling your leg with a poem. But nothing prepares you for the first flights of panache. For a moment, the audience doesn't know what to make of the rollicking procession of words. Then laughter erupts, and erupts after every line, streams of pleasure flowing back to the poet as applause. Later will come the sorrows and troubles of his roots in the tragic land that has so borne the brunt of history. For now, your*

*imagination is fired by poetical mischief as delightful as the
laughter of leprechauns dancing in the forest.*

*Let's begin with your poem "Symposium." It had the
audience in stitches.*

Symposium

You can lead a horse to water but you can't make it hold
its nose to the grindstone and hunt with the hounds.
Every dog has a stitch in time. Two heads? You've been sold
one good turn. One good turn deserves a bird in the hand.

A bird in the hand is better than no bread.
To have your cake is to pay Paul.
Make hay while you can still hit the nail on the head.
For want of a nail the sky might fall.

People in glass houses can't see the wood
for the new broom. Rome wasn't built between two stools.
Empty vessels wait for no man.

A hair of the dog is a friend indeed.
There's no fool like the fool
who's shot his bolt. There's no smoke after the horse is
    gone.

The audience loved it. But the poem makes no sense. Is that why they were laughing?

There's a great tradition in poetry of the nonsense poem, and I hope my little effort at playing on words plugs into that tradition. A symposium, as you know, was originally a philosophical discussion taking place over a glass of wine. Or, in the case of the speaker of this poem, maybe two glasses.

It's an example, for me, of the importance of hearing poets read their poems in their own voices. Listening to your Irish lilt makes me think of Sandburg's "verbs quivering, nouns echoing."

Well, that's one of the terrific things about coming to a festival like this. You get this electricity flowing back and forth between the audience and the poet, and you feel poetry really engaging people. I think this is why people today want the video, they want the audiocassette. They want to hear the poem. And that actually is a wonderful thing. I think it's wonderful that poetry is perhaps reaching a somewhat wider audience. I just think we need to keep in perspective that it needn't necessarily be a huge audience. Poetry has never been a particularly popular sport. The truth is, John Donne was read by a very small number of people, and they were people at court. Byron himself describes how he awoke one morning to find himself famous—on the strength of selling five hundred books of poetry! That's still a lot, by the way.

If he were around today, I'm sure we would get a flamboyant performance. Let me ask, how should we listen to a poem?

Test it on your inner ear. You've heard that phrase before. Some poems—most, perhaps—are written more for the eye than the ear. But the ear is the main test of a poem. So speak it inwardly or aloud to yourself. The tradition of reading inwardly, silently, is a comparatively recent thing. Until a few hundred years ago most people couldn't read, so others had to read for them.

Some people can hear the music of a poem in their heads, as they read. I need to hear poems aloud. Do you say them aloud to yourself as you're writing?

At some level. I don't necessarily speak them as I write, but they're spoken inwardly, as it were. That certainly is a major test in terms of the rhythm from line to line. And it's what's happening from line to line that's central to the whole activity. It's one of the distinctions between verse and prose. I can't remember who came up with this waggish distinction, but I like it: that what happens in a line of poetry is akin to what happens to the line drive of a golf ball. It's driven, driven on and on; there's an ongoing force about it. Now, this metaphor will break down almost immediately, as metaphors do. So let's change the metaphor. Think of a line of poetry more akin to a squash ball. That is to say, there's some notion of containment, of bouncing off walls, of hitting that limit and coming back again. You wrestle with this sort of thing when you're writing; you try to hear how the lines sound. How does one line come to an end? What turns it? And does the next one move the reader forward? The juncture where lines end, meet, and turn is critical. That's what the word *verse* is about. What does it mean to *versify* something? It means you arrange words by a metrical pattern, a line or a stanza. Verse is about coming around the corner. There has to be a reason why you come around that corner and keep going on.

The same thing happens in filmmaking. You choose the flow of a film, shot by shot. Yet good producers can "see" the film in their mind's eye even as they're working on it frame by frame. In the same way a poet "speaks" the poem inwardly is that what you're saying?

Yes, and one attempts to make it look natural, of course, to look as if it happened with great immediacy and ease. When you are putting together your film on the poetry festival, I'm sure you'll want to edit it, cut it, so it seems seamless and effortless and has a logic to it. That's the art of it. It's the same with poetry. The time that goes into making something look easy and natural is what we're talking about. And poets do it line by line. At least I do.

You certainly do it with "The Boundary Commission." The language is like the river carrying me along.

The Boundary Commission

You remember that village where the border ran
Down the middle of the street,
With the butcher and baker in different states?
Today he remarked how a shower of rain

Had stopped so cleanly across Golightly's lane
It might have been a wall of glass
That had toppled over. He stood there, for ages,
To wonder which side, if any, he should be on.

What was in your mind when you wrote, "He stood there, for ages / To wonder which side, if any, he should be on"?

What I'm interested in doing, usually, is writing poems

with very clear, translucent surfaces. But if you look at them again, there are other things happening under the surface. That poem began with a very concrete image of the line across a road that represented the edge or limit of a shower of rain. And it was quite an astonishing thing to see. A straight line crossing the road where the edge of this shower had fallen. I came upon this and was inspired by it as a wonderful image. In Ireland the border has been an ongoing question for us. So what starts with a natural act—a rain shower—becomes a kind of political poem. On one hand it's a poem about a shower of rain stopping across a road—a normal, everyday scene—but it moves on to raise questions about commitment, and the notion of taking sides, and the difficulties of taking sides. We're back to how the lines turn, one into another.

It made me think of my own forebears in Tennessee during the Civil War. Some chose the Confederacy, some chose the Union. And they were from the same county, fighting against each other. For a poet to turn such an event into a meditation of art, and with such economy of language, requires a certain temperament. Do you know how it happened in your life?

I really don't. We didn't have many books in the house, which is contrary to the experience of many poets. They're often surrounded by books. My mother was a schoolteacher, and we did have a respect for literacy in the family. And we owned an encyclopedia. I remember that I ended up reading the encyclopedia, looking for a plot. Maybe that's how I became interested in how words work. I think most people are engaged at one time or another by an interesting word. They must ask, "Where does that come from?" The poet can't just ask the question and stop there. The poet is in the habit of sitting down and musing over the question, making a note of some moment of clarity or vision, some metaphor or simile. I don't want to sound highfalutin about this, but so much of the process is about that habit of sitting down and working away. Many people seem to have an image of the poet as someone who's probably tousle-haired like myself, just walking along and being hit by lightning. There needs to be a little element of that, some aspect of what we conventionally think of as inspiration, something coming from beyond, a striking phrase, an image that hasn't quite occurred to anyone yet. But then you have to be willing to sit down and see what to do with it.

One of my teachers said that the creative process requires not only a lot of hard work but a habit of mind.

Yes, in a way. It's based on complete ignorance, you might say. At some level there's a deep aspect of unknowing about what you're doing. Only when you are open to the possibility of being taken somewhere you did not expect to end up is there going to be any spark or electricity or engagement. What produces that temperament? A knack, I suppose, for taking those little glimmers and moving them around until they interact and you discover that "my love is like a red, red rose." Right now I'm looking over your shoulder at that lichen on the tree bark beyond you. It reminds me of a skin condition. Many people will see that, even have that insight, and leave it at that. The poet has that little glimpse, as it were, and thinks: That may be useful someday. You make a note of it and you let it settle— the idea of bark on the tree with a skin condition. By the way, I don't think that's a metaphor or symbol that's going to set the world on fire. But the point is that at the heart of the exercise you are trying to bring two unlike things together.

Do you have your audience—listeners and readers—in mind when you're creating a poem?

I don't think that's the main reason you write poetry. You make your work accessible, but you write poetry to try and make sense of your life. If you do that, you trust that others may take the opportunity, if they're willing, to listen in, as it were, overhearing what you have to say.

I know it sounds a bit strange, but one of the reasons I write is that I'm kind of slow at things and it takes me a long time to discover through the act of writing what it is that is trying to get said through me. And this is difficult. Each stage of a poem represents some kind of failure. It's as if you haven't done it quite right at the time, and you think: Next time around I'll get it right. And next time you feel as if you were sitting down for the very first time to write that poem you've already started. It's the urge to do this again and again that makes people continue to do it. W. B. Yeats had a wonderful phrase. He said a man—and had he lived in this era, he would have said a man or a woman—dabbles in verses and they become his life. You just become absorbed in how words work, making them work for you. If you're very lucky, those words will occasionally make some music. And that takes over your life.

One reviewer recently wrote of what he called "the joyous quality" in your poems—the notes of affirmation you sound. And he wondered if this is deliberate, if coming from Northern Ireland, with its long history of violence, accounts for a decision on your part to sing a different tune.

I have tried in some of my poems to make sense of what has been happening in Northern Ireland for my own sake, if for no other. A citizen of Ireland has to take some responsibility for trying to make sense of the senseless, and so does a poet. I'm amazed—and amused, perhaps—to see the extent to which so many politicians in Ireland actually do have a sense of what various poets have written about the situation there. When President Clinton was in Ireland a couple of times back, he quoted from a number of Irish poets, and I don't think he was doing it just to do it. Poems can put a microscope to a situation. One of the things poetry does at its best is to be true to some small detail of a place and a time and a political situation, not offering a solution but offering a way into—I hesitate to use the word *verity* because it sounds so grandiose—but offering a way into the core of the tragedy, the heart of the matter.

Let me ask you about your poem about Joseph Plunkett Ward. I was struck by how the protagonist carried with him remembrances of his first experiences in school.

Oh, yes. That's "Anseo." The title is the first word of Irish that most of us learned, if we learned any at all, in school.

Anseo

When the Master was calling the roll
At the primary school in Collegelands,
You were meant to call back *Anseo*

And raise your hand
As your name occurred.
Anseo, meaning here, here and now,
All present and correct,
Was the first word of Irish I spoke.
The last name on the ledger
Belonged to Joseph Mary Plunkett Ward
And was followed, as often as not,
By silence, knowing looks,
A nod and a wink, the Master's droll
'And where's our little Ward-of-court?'

I remember the first time he came back
The Master had sent him out
Along the hedges
To weigh up for himself and cut
A stick with which he would be beaten.
After a while, nothing was spoken;
He would arrive as a matter of course
With an ash-plant, a salley-rod.
Or, finally, the hazel-wand
He had whittled down to a whip-lash,
Its twist of red and yellow lacquers
Sanded and polished,
And altogether so delicately wrought
That he had engraved his initials on it.

I last met Joseph Mary Plunkett Ward
In a pub just over the Irish border.
He was living in the open,
In a secret camp
On the other side of the mountain.
He was fighting for Ireland,
Making things happen.
And he told me, Joe Ward,
Of how he had risen through the ranks
To Quartermaster, Commandant:
How every morning at parade
His volunteers would call back *Anseo*
And raise their hands
As their names occurred.

As you read, some old lines come to mind, "Verse is not written, it is bled." I had a similar response listening to "The Sightseers." Tell me about that experience.

Well, when we were living in Ireland, it seemed that for a long time my parents had organized a little outing every Sunday afternoon, a little sightseeing trip for us. And I can tell you we were not going to poetry festivals up the road. We restricted ourselves to visits to graveyards. My parents had moved about ten miles away, which is a lunar distance in Ireland, and they had a very wide circle of acquaintances, many of whom had by now passed on. And they went to pay their respects to quite a number of graveyards within ten miles of home. It can get kind of tedious. We'd wish for a change in the routine, but we relied for a long time on a particular uncle for the ride because we had no car for our own, so we didn't have a lot of flexibility. Then we finally got a car of our own, and on our first trip with it, we visited a roundabout, a traffic circle. I think it was the first traffic circle in Ireland—certainly in Northern Ireland. We'd heard reports about it, and there was nothing to do until we went to experience it ourselves. I remember quite vividly driving up to it and cautiously driving round it until we got the hang of it, and then driving around and around it. Before I read, I should tell you that the B-Specials were the auxiliary force of the Royal Ulster Constabulary, and they were capable of some pretty bad behavior. The sash I refer to in the poem is the Orange song "The Sash My Father Wore." So much for an extremely long introduction to what is a shortish poem.

The Sightseers

My father and mother, my brother and sister
and I, with uncle Pat, our dour best-loved uncle,
had set out that Sunday afternoon in July
in his broken-down Ford

not to visit some graveyard—one died of shingles,
one of fever, another's knees turned to jelly—
but the brand-new roundabout at Ballygawley,
the first in mid Ulster.

Uncle Pat was telling us how the B-Specials
had stopped him one night somewhere near Ballygawley
and smashed his bicycle

and made him sing the Sash and curse the Pope of Rome.
They held a pistol so hard against his forehead
there was still the mark of an O when he got home.

You have this knack for the telling anecdote plucked from the moment, sometimes it's from the here and now rather than the past. I'm thinking of "The Train."

Yes. Well, we moved recently, and one of the reasons we moved had to do with a series of interruptions—two or three times in the course of a night—from a train that would come rattling and roaring and shrieking through about a mile away. I do not know why it felt obliged to make this terrific racket—perhaps to warn an unsuspecting soul at a level crossing that they were on the way. It turns out that more often than not the train was carrying Tropicana orange juice.

The Train

I've been trying, my darling, to explain
to myself how it is that some freight train
loaded with ballast so a track may rest
easier in its bed should be what's roused

us both from ours, tonight as every night,
despite its being miles off and despite
our custom of putting to the very
back of the mind all that's customary

and then, since it takes forever to pass
with its car after car of coal and gas
and salt and wheat and rails and railway ties,

how it seems determined to give the lie
to the notion, my darling,
that we, not it, might be the constant thing.

*Do you know why the passing train triggered this
response?*

As usual, I really didn't know what I was doing in
writing the poem, but in trying to describe it, the train
came to stand against the idea of a relationship, which
we usually think of as being long-lasting. The train

threatens to last even longer. I hope that a reader will be disturbed in some way by having wandered into and through the poem and will come out the other end changed in some way. Not necessarily changed in a dramatic way, but in some small way. So that, for example, the reader will never think of a train in quite the same way. My process is very simple in that sense. Since I don't know what I am doing, there is a chance the reader won't know what I am doing also. So it is possible that something interesting might happen. Keats used the term "negative capability" to encourage the writer not to go seeking after conventional reason, the conventionally rational, but to give himself over to uncertainties, mysteries, and doubts.

MARGE PIERCY

*T*HE EARLY MORNING *light appears in the window like a penitent sinner eager for sanctuary within the white-steepled church. By the time the sun's rays reach the hand-wrought stenciling high on the walls, the pews are filling with people. Whether they are repentant sinners or not is impossible to know, and immaterial. They are poetry lovers, and if in their obsession they have sinned at all, it is more likely to have been some dalliance with mixed metaphors, a weakness for a hackneyed pun, or the seduction of a flirtatious alliteration. This old church has heard far more and forgiven far worse. Built in 1859, on the eve of the Civil War, it maintains the only continuous life of all the buildings in the restored village of Waterloo. During the Dodge Festival, it has become a favorite for morning poetry. The natural light on the venerable walls and*

the close proximity of poet to listener allow what poetry invites, the intimacy of communion. Marge Piercy reads her poem "The Chuppah," and I am fascinated by the juxtaposition of images. Here in this United Methodist Church—the architectural and theological epitome of traditional Protestantism—the poet of the moment is not only Jewish but a political radical. In the 1960s, Marge Piercy was a student activist for civil rights and marched against the Vietnam War. Joining the women's movement, she challenged men who rule society with "the armed brain and the barbed penis and the club." Her novels and poems abound in women "who are not young, not beautiful, not white, not rich, not married, or about to be." Some critics may wince at her politics, but no one can doubt whose voice is speaking, or that the language comes from a fully engaged life. Not that politics is her only subject. She writes about planting tomatoes, making love, remodeling the kitchen, and dying. Her avid followers know that she can be just as tough about herself—and as humorous—as about the world's absurdities. At heart, Marge Piercy is a utopian, possessing what Margaret Atwood describes as "a view of human possibility—harmony between the sexes, among races, and between humankind and nature—that makes the present state of affairs clearly unacceptable by comparison." Now I know why it seems so natural for Piercy to be reading here in this old church. The Jewish prophets and the founder of the Christian faith alike took on the powers-that-be, honored fugitive women and other outcasts, and relished weddings where miracles happen.

The Chuppah

The chuppah stands on four poles.
The home has its four corners.
The chuppah stands on four poles.
The marriage stands on four legs.
Four points loose the winds
that blow on the walls of the house,
the south wind that brings the warm rain,
the east wind that brings the cold rain,
the north wind that brings the cold sun
and the snow, the long west wind
bringing the weather off the far plains.

Here we live open to the seasons.
Here the winds caress and cuff us
contrary and fierce as bears.
Here the winds are caught and snarling
in the pines, a cat in a net clawing
breaking twigs to fight loose.
Here the winds brush your face
soft in the morning as feathers
that float down from a dove's breast.

Here the moon sails up out of the ocean
dripping like a just washed apple.
Here the sun wakes us like a baby.
Therefore the chuppah has no sides.

It is not a box.
It is not a coffin.
It is not a dead end.
Therefore the chuppah has no walls.
We have made a home together
open to the weather of our time.
We are mills that turn in the winds of struggle
converting fierce energy into bread.

The canopy is the cloth of our table
where we share fruit and vegetables
of our labor, where our care for the earth
comes back and we take its body in ours.

The canopy is the cover of our bed
where our bodies open their portals wide,
where we eat and drink the blood
of our love, where the skin shines red
as a swallowed sunrise and we burn
in one furnace of joy molten as steel
and the dream is flesh and flower.

O my love O my love we dance
under the chuppah standing over us
like an animal on its four legs,
like a table on which we set our love
as a feast, like a tent
under which we work
not safe but no longer solitary
in the searing heat of our time.

How did that poem come to be?

My husband, Ira Wood, and I were married by a wonderful woman rabbi, Debra Hachen, who invited us to join in creating the ceremony. So we both wrote poems for it—the only poems my husband ever wrote. One prominent feature of the Jewish ceremony is the canopy held on four poles over the couple—in this case, it was a shawl I had given my mother, who had died the year before. The chuppah, with its elements of tent and table, provided the imagery for the poem. The elements of repetition in the poem are intended to heighten the experience and the sense of joyful excitement in the celebration. Finding the meaning in the public symbol is not conscious but comes through observing and connecting: what has four legs (an animal, a table), what do open sides suggest (an unfinished structure), what has a cover put over it (a bed, a table)? Thus the chuppah poem. The chuppah becomes an emblem of the kind of marriage we sought, with themes of tradition and liberation.

I've been pleased that other people now use this poem in their own weddings. My husband and I took part in the wedding of a friend recently—we both read poems— and a man came up to me after the ceremony and asked, "Is your poem part of the Jewish ritual now?" And I said, "Not necessarily!" "Well," he said, "I've been to two weddings in two weeks and heard it both times."

You are adding to the tradition! Do you find yourself more interested in Jewish rituals at this stage of your life?

When my mother died and I said Kaddish for her for the next year, I stumbled through the experience because I didn't know any Hebrew. In our family the boys were taught Hebrew but the girls were not. So I was just mouthing these nonsense syllables. The siddurs or prayer books that have been written in English are dreadful. The Hebrew is beautiful, but the English is just awful! So I determined to learn Hebrew, and that led to my becoming very involved again in Judaism. I've been trying to create an appropriate English translation so people who don't use Hebrew, which means most English-speaking Jews now, can have a language to pray in that will mean something to them, that will move them.

There's a difference between writing my usual poems and writing liturgy. Liturgy is a hard discipline. Poems intended to be used as liturgy will usually be said by a group. They have to have a simplicity of structure, which is usually determined by the needs of the service. They absolutely must work out loud, and they should be comfortable to the rhythms of spoken speech. I also found I had to avoid overly personal material and try to select imagery that most of the people likely to use that particular piece would find fitted them. It was an interesting discipline for a poet.

Is religion influencing your poetry at some subterranean level?

Well, the Bible is poetic. And I find what I'm doing very centering. Everything to me is connected—religion, the body, politics, our relation to each other and all other living beings, the environment. Life is of a piece. To me it's all one vision, and poetry is at the center. I don't divide things into categories. I don't believe that if you write about religion you can't write political poems, or that you can write love poems but you can't write God poems. What's revealing to me is that through poetry many people attain consciousness about themselves and their place in society. I keep discovering that my own constituency is so diverse and scattered. There are people who relate to the Jewish poems, people who relate to the nature poems, to the political poems, the feminist poems. I've been amazed at the number of unions that tell me how helpful "To be of use" is to them in their organizing work.

To be of use

The people I love the best
jump into work head first
without dallying in the shallows
and swim off with sure strokes almost out of sight.
They seem to become natives of that element,
the black sleek heads of seals
bouncing like half-submerged balls.

I love people who harness themselves, an ox to a heavy cart,
who pull like water buffalo, with massive patience,
who strain in the mud and the muck to move things forward,
who do what has to be done, again and again.

I want to be with people who submerge
in the task, who go into the fields to harvest
and work in a row and pass the bags along,
who are not parlor generals and field deserters

but move in a common rhythm
when the food must come in or the fire be put out.

The work of the world is common as mud.
Botched, it smears the hands, crumbles to dust.
But the thing worth doing well done
has a shape that satisfies, clean and evident.
Greek amphoras for wine or oil,
Hopi vases that held corn, are put in museums
but you know they were made to be used.
The pitcher cries for water to carry
and a person for work that is real.

*That's a very striking line—"The pitcher cries for water
to carry / and a person for work that is real." What inspired
this poem?*

It's about real work. I just looked around at all the
people who support me. Somebody made this jacket I'm
wearing. Somebody produced the materials for it.
Somebody grew the food I eat—well, I grow some of
my own food in a huge vegetable garden, but I don't
have chickens and the eggs. Somebody made your
glasses. There's so much labor in everything. This
poem is my way of giving back, of acknowledging the
people I depend on.

Do you remember how you went about writing this poem?

You can date the poem by the water buffalo. That takes us back to the Vietnam War and to the images of peasants in the fields with water buffalo being strafed and napalmed. In my ordinary life these days, I probably wouldn't think of water buffalo any longer. I might think of turtles or spiders for patience. The ox in the poem came from a visit I made to the Organic State Fair in Maine, from watching an oxen pull. I was enormously impressed by the animals there, the vast pigs with their dignity, the enormous, powerful oxen, the clever goats. I talk with animals a lot.

I am an intensely curious person, nosy, insatiable. As a poet, everything you experience, whether personally or vicariously or virtuously or virtually, for that matter, is your stuff. Imagery can't really be taught. You can lecture about the different kinds of imagery in different sorts of poems, but the truth is, imagery is the most personal core of a poet. What you know and what you feel becomes your imagery. The more you actually see—how carefully you look at an opossum or a wildflower or the way light strikes water or hair; the more you actually listen to the natural and manufactured sounds of our world; the more you know about what the shape of a bird's beak means about what it eats, or what the weeds growing in a field tell you about the soil and its history—then the more stuff you will have within you that will rise and suggest itself as imagery. You have to stay open and curious and keep learning as you go. Poems come from a whole variety of sources. When you're younger, you believe in inspiration. As you get older, you believe most in receptivity and work.

That's what you're reminding young people of in your poem "For the young who want to."

The poem is not, of course, just for young people. It's really for anybody starting out in any of the arts at any age. A woman came to me and said, "I'm fifty. Can I still be a poet?" The answer is yes, but it takes work.

For the young who want to

Talent is what they say
you have after the novel
is published and favorably
reviewed. Beforehand what
you have is a tedious
delusion, a hobby like knitting.

Work is what you have done
after the play is produced
and the audience claps.

Before that friends keep asking
when you are planning to go
out and get a job.

Genius is what they know you
had after the third volume
of remarkable poems. Earlier
they accuse you of withdrawing,
ask why you don't have a baby,
call you a bum.

The reason people want M.F.A.'s,
take workshops with fancy names
when all you can really
learn is a few techniques,
typing instructions and some-
body else's mannerisms

is that every artist lacks
a license to hang on the wall
like your optician, your vet
proving you may be a clumsy sadist
whose fillings fall into the stew
but you're certified a dentist.

The real writer is one
who really writes. Talent

is an invention like phlogiston
after the fact of fire.
Work is its own cure. You have to
like it better than being loved.

I am curious about the word phlogiston. *I've never heard of it before.*

It comes from the history of science. I've always been fascinated by science—after all, I married two scientists before marrying a writer. When I was young, I thought they were the people who knew something I didn't. I'm still fascinated by biology and astronomy, anthropology and physics. Phlogiston was a pre-nineteenth-century explanation for why things burned: People said things burned because they contained phlogiston. It always struck me as the perfect example of a false explanation. You are said to write good poems because you have talent, and the proof you have talent is that you write good poems. That's just not satisfactory.

Some critics say we don't need to know about a poet's life to appreciate the poet's work, and in one sense I understand that. But if we are going to understand how imagination affects creativity, it seems to me that we need to explore the actual circumstances of a life and how the poet interprets them. For example, your poems often treat the grittiness of life. Does that come from your own experiences? I know you had to support yourself by being a secretary, a switchboard operator, a clerk. Were those defining years for your poetry?

No more so than growing up in the center of Detroit and losing a good friend to heroin when I was fifteen. No more than being in the movement against the Vietnam War and experiencing the violence of the government's willingness to use force against people who dissent. No more than packing a woman with ice so she wouldn't bleed to death because a doctor wouldn't help her when abortions were illegal. No more so than being shot at in Mexico and seeing the student leaders there eviscerated on the lawn of the university. I've had a lot of experiences in my life. I've been a lot of places and done a lot of things. They all inform who I am and where I live. I grow fourteen kinds of tomatoes. I grow yellow tomatoes, orange tomatoes, purple tomatoes, pink tomatoes, red tomatoes, little tomatoes, big tomatoes. That's real and that also informs my poetry. We have been living in times in which human cruelty is all around us. Yet the world is very beautiful. As we're sitting here, there are geese waddling by—a whole family of geese, and they're beautiful.

And over there the trucks on Highway 80 are roaring by—

—with their own reality. And the woods around us have been dug up and replaced with rows of identical houses stretching away for a mile or so. All of this is real. To be a poet is to open your eyes to everything around you. I love the beauty of the world, but I get angry at the cruelty in the world. How can we not get angry at the tremendous cruelty that is built into our system?

You once said the defense of the status quo is as political as an attack on it. Would you agree that the majority of people today apparently feel pretty good about the status quo?

But what about the people who are not polled, whose voices are not heard? The rich are still indifferent, there's racism throughout society, and the powerful still divide and conquer the working class. From the third grade on, women are trained to mistrust their natural bodies and to try to make them conform with body types belonging to two percent of the population. I said in one of my poems that we treat our own bodies as "gardens to be weeded, dogs to be trained." According to the polls, a great many of us find our closest relationship with characters on TV or with our pets. Very few people feel any sense of security about the future, no matter how well they may be doing right now.

In many countries it's expected that poets will speak to the controversies of the day. They often write the op-ed pieces. They speak truth to power. They write poems like these middle stanzas of your poem "A gift of light."

From *A gift of light*

On those Washington avenues that resemble
emperor-sized cemeteries, vast Roman mausoleum
after mausoleum where Justice and Health
are budgeted out of existence for the many,
men who smell of cologne are pushing pins
across maps. It is time to attach the left
again, it is time for a mopping up
operation against those of us who opposed
their wars too soon, too seriously, too long.
It is time to silence the shrill voices
of women whose demands incommode men
with harems of illpaid secretaries, men
for whom industries purr, men who buy death wholesale.
Today some are released from prison and others
are sucked in. Those who would not talk

to grand juries are boxed from the light
to grow fungus on their brains and those
who talked receive a message it is time
to talk again.

I try hard to be simple, to remember always
to ask for whom what is done is done.
Who gets and who loses? Who pays
and who rakes off the profit? Whose
life is shortened? Whose heat
is shut off? Whose children end
shooting up or shot in the streets?

I try to remember to ask simple questions,
I try to remember to love my friends and fight
my enemies. But their faces are hidden
in the vaults of banks, their names are inscribed
on the great plains by strip mining and you can
only read the script from Mars. Their secret
wills are encoded in the computers that mind
nuclear submarines armed with the godheads
of death. . . .

. . .

Let no one doubt, no onlookers, no heirs
of our agonies, how much I have loved
what I have loved. Flying back

from Washington, I saw the air steely
bright out to the huge bell of horizon.
I leaned against the plane window, cheek
to the plastic, crooning to see the curve
of the Cape hooking out in the embrace
of the water, to see the bays, the tidal
rivers, the intricate web of marshes,
the whole body of this land like beautiful
lace, like a fraying bronze net laid
on the glittering fish belly of the sea.

. . .

Can poetry like that make a difference in a country so content with itself?

Not everyone is so content. Listen to the rhetoric of the militia in the West. Read the letters to the editor. Lots of people are angry and just can't figure out where to aim their anger. We forget how to do anything political. Every generation has to start all over again—people have to figure out what's happened, but you have to start with two, three at a time, and organize. In the meantime, we need the poems—if not for the politicians then for the people the politicians ignore.

So exactly how do you want a poem to be useful?

I want my poems to give voice to something in the experience of a life. To find ourselves spoken for in art gives dignity to our pain, our anger, our losses. We can hear what we hope for and what we most fear in the small release of a cadence's utterance. I just hope that readers will find poems that speak for and to them. I hope they'll stick a poem up on the bathroom mirror, pass it to a friend on some good or troubled occasion, put it over their computer or on the refrigerator, remember some lines that encourage them, help them cope with pain, anger, with their dreams. The farther you are from the centers of power in this society, the less likely you are to find validation of your experiences, your insights and ideas, your life. It is more important to you to find in art that validation, that respect for your experiences that no minority except the thin, white, and wealthy can count on.

In a way, every poem is a leap of faith, isn't it? You trust it will find its way to a receptive heart.

You never know when your poem will come to someone's rescue. I can tell you that poetry spoke to me when I was just a street kid from Detroit. It was validation that I wasn't crazy, that what I felt wasn't bizarre, that I wasn't totally nutty. Poems told me there were other people who felt the way I felt. That was validation for the person I was. Poems can mean survival. Let me give you an example. If you're female in this society, culture tells you that you've had it if you're not twenty-two, blond, and weigh about ninety-two pounds. Then, even if you are twenty-two, blond, and weigh ninety-two pounds, you're still going to fail because you're going to get old. Women are destined to age into failure even if when they're young they are what society defines as perfect. Poems about women who are not twenty-two, blond, and ninety-two pounds can remind us of reality.

And what about men. Are you still angry with men?

At mechanistic, thoughtless, narcissistic men, yes; men with no concern for other people or the natural world.

You have written so much about women's lives. Were there women who especially influenced you?

My grandmother, for one. She was a wonderful woman. She didn't think of herself as educated, but she gave me an enormous sense of the female side of Judaism. She had long hair, which she would braid and unbraid and it would tumble down like Rapunzel's. She was also a woman of great inner beauty. She would have told you she was ignorant, but she spoke five languages—Lithuanian, Russian, Polish, Yiddish, and English—and she had a tremendous sense of story, especially in Yiddish. She and my mother gave me my own sense of story. Her husband, my grandfather, was a very erudite man. He was a labor organizer, and he was murdered. He was organizing the bakery workers and his head was bashed in, leaving my grandmother and their nine children—my mother was one of them—in dire poverty. My mother was not allowed to finish the tenth grade. She was sent to work. She had no skills. She was never anything but a chambermaid. She was strong in some ways and completely helpless in others. She couldn't leave a bad marriage. She could not drive a car. She had tiny little feet and could hardly walk. On the other hand, she was very gifted with animals and birds. It was observing these contradictions that taught me a whole lot about women's lives. She was a combination of tremendous gifts and power and tremendous weakness and vulnerability and anger. She made me observant. For her it was absolutely important that you notice things, that you pay attention, that you not walk around, as she would put it, with your head in the clouds.

In one of the poems you read last night there's a line: "Attention is love."

It's true. I've often thought that in my poems I was speaking for my mother, whose life was so painful and so starved of so many things she wanted and needed—the affection that she craved or the dignity that she felt she had in her but that the world did not accord her.

Did she live long enough to know you had become a poet?

Yes. My father never read anything—he just wasn't interested in my work—but my mother read my poems. She liked my poetry much better than my fiction because she thought you should talk about sex but you shouldn't write it down. But the poetry she liked, and we became very close toward the end.

Let's close with "For strong women."

For strong women

A strong woman is a woman who is straining.
A strong woman is a woman standing
on tiptoe and lifting a barbell
while trying to sing Boris Godunov.
A strong woman is a woman at work
cleaning out the cesspool of the ages,
and while she shovels, she talks about
how she doesn't mind crying, it opens

the ducts of the eyes, and throwing up
develops the stomach muscles, and
she goes on shoveling with tears
in her nose.

A strong woman is a woman in whose head
a voice is repeating, I told you so,
ugly, bad girl, bitch, nag, shrill, witch,
ballbuster, nobody will ever love you back,
why aren't you feminine, why aren't
you soft, why aren't you quiet, why
aren't you dead?

A strong woman is a woman determined
to do something others are determined
not be done. She is pushing up on the bottom
of a lead coffin lid. She is trying to raise
a manhole cover with her head, she is trying
to butt her way through a steel wall.
Her head hurts. People waiting for the hole
to be made say, hurry, you're so strong.

A strong woman is a woman bleeding
inside. A strong woman is a woman making
herself strong every morning while her teeth
loosen and her back throbs. Every baby,
a tooth, midwives used to say, and now

every battle a scar. A strong woman
is a mass of scar tissue that aches
when it rains and wounds that bleed
when you bump them and memories that get up
in the night and pace in boots to and fro.

A strong woman is a woman who craves love
like oxygen or she turns blue choking.
A strong woman is a woman who loves
strongly and weeps strongly and is strongly
terrified and has strong needs. A strong woman is strong
in words, in action, in connection, in feeling;
she is not strong as a stone but as a wolf
suckling her young. Strength is not in her, but she
enacts it as the wind fills a sail.

What comforts her is others loving
her equally for the strength and for the weakness
from which it issues, lightning from a cloud.
Lightning stuns. In rain, the clouds disperse.
Only water of connection remains,
flowing through us. Strong is what we make
each other. Until we are all strong together,
a strong woman is a woman strongly afraid.

It's not very complicated, the reason for that poem.
The deepest spiritual insights tell us that we live feel-

ingly. We live experiencing. We have to know how connected we are. It's quite remarkable, the very strange notion of the self today. We think the self stops right here. But my self doesn't stop here. It flows out into the people I love, into the people I have loved, the people I come from, the people I speak to. Sometimes, in dream or in vision, we encounter each other without boundaries. Being strong means being strong together.

ROBERT PINSKY

*A*MERICANS STILL HAVE *a hard time with the title
"Poet Laureate." It's so, well, so English—invented by the
Crown and bestowed on Ben Jonson by James I in 1616.
And all those names of Poets Laureate that Mrs. Hughes
reeled off in class: Pye, Dryden, Southey, Wordsworth,
Tennyson, Masefield—so very, very English. Didn't we
mount a revolution to rid ourselves of English titles? When
Americans did begin to call poets to the service of the Repub-
lic sixty years ago, we dubbed them "poetry consultant to the
Library of Congress," a real clunker of a title, as if they
were business school graduates called in to reorganize the
library's card system. Gradually we matured and now
acknowledge the holder of the office as Poet Laureate of the
United States.*

Here is the incumbent reading his poem "To Television."
You can hardly get more American than that! Robert Pinsky
doesn't look English either. He looks, let's face it, he looks
New Jersey. He can sound New Jersey, too, especially when
he's regaling an audience with tales of his bootlegging
grandfather and other assorted saints and rascals from his
hometown of Long Branch. Imagine! A Poet Laureate from
Long Branch, New Jersey—with its bars, ethnic oaths, and
kids gawking at the circus freaks in Flanagan's Field. The
grandees—Ulysses S. Grant, Diamond Jim Brady, Lillian
Russell—came to breathe the ocean air, and although they
stayed only for the summer, they left their mark on town
lore. A kid growing up in Long Branch could hear all the
stories, sounds, buzzing tongues, and clacking wheels and
run them through the Mixmaster of his imagination. Come
to think of it, what better place to spawn an American Poet
Laureate? This one has taken his measure of the world's fine
poets and made them his mentors; his translation of Dante's
Inferno *has even become a bestseller. But there's something*
so undeniably American about Robert Pinsky that you half-
expect him to break out in "The Star-Spangled Banner" as
he reads, or see Old Glory unfurl behind him. Not surpris-
ingly, one of his books is entitled An Explanation of Amer-
ica. *King Jimmy the First must be shaking his head in*
wonder—may he rest in peace—that democracy now claims
the title.

Somehow I wasn't surprised when you told the young people in your workshop that inspiration comes from common things like shopping malls and television.

All of my poems are about the same thing: the fact that there's history in everything. Everything comes partly from something else, some other place. So for the poet, the shopping mall here in New Jersey is as historic as Florence, Italy. If Florence looks more historical to us, maybe our perception equipment is defective. Both places are outcomes of hundreds and thousands of years of natural history and tens of thousands of human history. So are you and I. My body and your body are the products of many, many experiences—kings and slaves and rapes and love matches we don't know about. And our cultural history is equally dense and layered and unknown, so that everything is a haunted ruin—haunted because we sense the past and a ruin because we know only fragments about it.

What does this mean for the poet?

The poet's challenge is to find something in culture that isn't already defined as poetic and make it poetic. I believe that before Baudelaire and Dickens made the city poetic, it wasn't as poetic. The artist transformed the commonplace of the day. So that the city of Carol Reed's *The Third Man* or the city of *Blade Runner* is a descendant of the sensibility of Dickens and Baudelaire and others who discovered the poetic in the industrial city—the smoke, the dust, the winding streets. There's a process of the human imagination's taking in its surroundings and discovering how to make art of them. What could be more unpromising than a steel oil drum? Smells bad, gets rusty, it's not attractive. But people took the steel oil drum and made music from it—a new *kind* of music. The same with poets. Our challenge is not to write a Wordsworth poem about a lake. You could, of course, see the lake in a different way. But the lake and the mountains are already poetic. Wordsworth made them poetic. And the sun going down over the Seine is poetic. Baudelaire made it poetic. If there's something in your experience that moves you but seems without poetry, your challenge is to make it poetic. For modern Americans, the shopping mall is what the lake was for Wordsworth: a significant, familiar locale. It's the result of history. If you can understand the language that people there are using, the history of the logos and the brand names and the graphic art styles of the store signs, the dyes in the fabrics, where those fabrics are made—Korea or Costa Rica—if you can understand all of this, you can find inspiration in it. The challenge for the writer is to take what does not seem automatically part of the realm of art and to make art out of it.

Including television?

Certainly including television. I don't know if you've noticed, but television's quite powerful.

I notice it's powerful, but poetic?

Well, it's not always poetic—that's very good news for poets, because it remains poetic raw material, since no poet has yet made it a poetic subject.

Wordsworth would have a hard time with it, but Pinsky, maybe not.

Maybe you're underestimating Wordsworth!

So why did you write a poem about television?

I can give you a personal answer. When I was a kid, we dealt with unhappiness in my family partly by escaping to television. From a very early age, for whatever reason, I became scornful of our using television as a painkiller. Then, somewhere down the road I realized there's a lot I love in television. Sid Caesar's audacity and range and daring, in particular. He used all kinds of cultural materials from low to high—from the most stupid and banal to opera and foreign films and literature. And in seeing Jackie Robinson on television, I found another great hero.

On another level we have to respect television—its economic power, its hold over people. It's our environment, part scam, part authentic. If you live in the islands of the Pacific, you study the ocean. To ignore the ocean would be peculiar. If you live near a volcano, you're likely to write poems about a volcano. This is a powerful thing I live near—television—and I wanted to write about it.

To Television

Not a "window on the world"
But as we call you,
A box a tube

Terrarium of dreams and wonders.
Coffer of shades, ordained
Cotillion of phosphors
Or liquid crystal

Homey miracle, tub
Of acquiescence, vein of defiance.
Your patron in the pantheon would be Hermes

Raster dance,
Quick one, little thief, escort
Of the dying and comfort of the sick,

In a blue glow my father and little sister sat
Snuggled in one chair watching you
Their wife and mother was sick in the head
I scorned you and them as I scorned so much

Now I like you best in a hotel room,
Maybe minutes
Before I have to face an audience: behind
The doors of the armoire, box
Within a box—Tom & Jerry, or also brilliant
And reassuring, Oprah Winfrey.

Thank you, for I watched, I watched
Sid Caesar speaking French and Japanese not
Through knowledge but imagination,
His quickness, and Thank you, I watched live
Jackie Robinson stealing

Home, the image—O strung shell—enduring
Fleeter than light like these words we
Remember in: they too are winged
At the helmet and ankles.

*When you write about television you're writing about a
phenomenon Americans have in common. Listening to you in
the workshop yesterday, I was reminded of something Stanley
Kunitz told me the other day. He said the democratic spirit of
a festival like this is indicative of one of the most important
revolutions in the history of modern poetry. So many people
with their stories to tell!*

There are two things you can say about poetry in that
regard. You don't need a lot of expensive equipment or
technology for it. All you need is a human body with a
voice inside it, and an imagination. The other thing
about poetry is that there's not a lot of money in it.
That can be beautiful, too. Poets remind me in some
ways of jazz musicians—people do it because they love
the art, they're just crazy about it. Like jazz, poetry
feeds other arts—creates ideas that find their way into
the mass arts. So I'm not surprised to see so many peo-
ple at a poetry festival like this. They're crazy about it.
Now, there's no automatic, institutional place in Amer-
ica where people love the art of poetry. There's not a
social class that considers poetry its property. And

there's no star value attached to the art the way there is in some other countries. So when I look around here and see young people as well as people my age and older—all of us thinking about the art I've given my life to—well, that's inspiring. That feels good. As you say, it's a very democratic thing. Poetry involves all these people you see around us, but it works on an individual scale, too. Poetry is an art embodied in one human voice. And without denigrating art on a mass scale—I love my television, my computer, my VCR—there's a particular craving and satisfaction available in an art form that is by its nature on an individual scale.

You say poetry is an art embodied in one human voice. How did you find your voice as a poet?

When I talk about a poetic voice I mean it literally—the thing that vibrates in my throat here, that I shape with the membranes in my mouth and my teeth. If you watch ten kids playing basketball, each of them employs a slightly different style. Everybody will throw the ball and move down court in a way that's a little bit different. It's an individual thing. So is the voice. We fall physically in love, I believe, with whatever activity expresses ourselves. That's what happened to me. I did it the way most musicians do it—by listening to older musicians. In my case, Yeats and Allen Ginsberg and

Emily Dickinson. When I would come across words like "Further in Summer than the Birds / Pathetic from the Grass / A minor Nation celebrates / Its unobtrusive Mass"—I thought that if I could say her words in my New Jersey baritone and have them sound good, I would be on my way to being able to say my own words.

Then it was sound that compelled you toward poetry.

Yes, there was a physical response. Don't you think this is true about almost any human interest? If you fall in love with a person, a cuisine, an animal, or a sport, in time you'll want to analyze it, know the history of it, and know what intelligent people think about it. But the first thing is—you like to pet the animal, eat the food, look at the person. After that primary experience comes intelligence. Ezra Pound says that poetry is a centaur. I take it to mean that in prose you try to hit a target with an arrow. In poetry you do the same thing, only you're riding a horse at the same time. And the horse is the human body, the physical part of the poem, the sound.

If that's the case, what am I to do as the listener?

Just three words: Read it aloud. Read it aloud. And don't worry about interpreting it, or emulating Gielgud. Just read it aloud to relish the consonants and vowels and the way the verbs and adjectives and nouns do their job. If the writer has got it right, you say aloud, "Love at the lips was touch / As sweet as I could bear; / And once that seemed too much; / I lived on air / That crossed me from sweet things / The flow of—was it musk / From hidden grapevine springs / Down hill at dusk?" and the sounds are coming out of your body. When you try it two or three times, you'll be hearing your voice.

So when you write, do you intend to produce a certain sound?

Well, I write with my voice. It's like improvising with jazz. Picture Edwin Arlington Robinson starting off with a short sentence—"She fears him and will always ask what fated her to choose him." Who can say whether he first thought about her fearing him or wondering what fated her. But the sound is there—*ya da ya da ya da ya da da*—as it is in jazz. You may be thinking about the chord structure, the harmonic structure, and the rhythm. You may be thinking about an idea you have and how it could be broken down into a sequence. But first, how does it sound?

Spoken like an old saxophonist! Did the world lose a first-class saxophonist when you chose poetry over jazz?

There's no question in my mind at all that the world lost a fourth-rate saxophonist when I became a poet. But you make the right connection. My whole life's work has been that of a frustrated saxophone player. I confess that I would abandon all my books, trade it all in, if I could play the way people I admire play. I do play with tapes, with electronic sidemen.

The saxophone is a very important symbol of culture to me. It's European in its origins, but black Americans took it over. Geniuses like Johnny Hodges, Lester Young, Coleman Hawkins, John Coltrane, and Dexter Gordon made it an American instrument, their instrument. I have a poem in which I try in certain passages to emulate the kinds of rhythms and harmonies and sounds they made, and that I wish I could make, with the horn. "Ginza Samba" is the title of an actual jazz tune written by Vincent Guaraldi and performed by him and many others, including Cal Tjader and Stan Getz.

Ginza Samba

A monosyllabic European called Sax
Invents a horn, walla whirledy wah, a kind of twisted
Brazen clarinet, but with its column of vibrating
Air shaped not in a cylinder but in a cone
Widening ever outward and bawaah spouting

Infinitely upward through an upturned
Swollen golden bell rimmed
Like a gloxinia flowering
In Sax's Belgian imagination

And in the unfathomable matrix
Of mothers and fathers as a genius graven
Humming into the cells of the body
Or cupped in the resonating grail
Of memory changed and exchanged
As in the trading of brasses,
Pearls and ivory, calicos and slaves,
Laborers and girls, two

Cousins in a royal family
Of Niger known as the Birds or Hawks.
In Christendom one cousin's child
Becomes a "favorite negro" ennobled
By decree of the Czar and founds
A great family, a line of generals,
Dandies and courtiers including the poet
Pushkin, killed in a duel concerning
His wife's honor, while the other cousin sails

In the belly of a slaveship to the port
Of Baltimore where she is raped
And dies in childbirth, but the infant

Will marry a Seminole and in the next
Chorus of time their child fathers
A great Hawk or Bird, with many followers
Among them this great-grandchild of the Jewish
Manager of a Pushkin estate, blowing

His American breath out into the wiggly
Tune uncurling its triplets and sixteenths—the Ginza
Samba of breath and brass, the reed
Vibrating as a valve, the aether, the unimaginable
Wires and circuits of an ingenious box
Here in my room in this house built
A hundred years ago while I was elsewhere:

It is like falling in love, the atavistic
Imperative of some one
Voice or face—the skill, the copper filament,
The golden bellful of notes twirling through
Their invisible element from
Rio to Tokyo and back again gathering
Speed in the variations as they tunnel
The twin haunted labyrinths of stirrup
And anvil echoing here in the hearkening
Instrument of my skull.

Now, what I try to do in poems is somewhere on the
line between speaking to you as I am now and creating

actual song. What I love when I say a poem is that it's a little bit like singing, a little bit like speaking.

Okay, let's take an example—your poem on the alphabet. Where did that come from?

I'm an abecedarian. When my mind is idling, it often goes to the alphabet, and it will give itself little puzzles to do with the letters. The alphabet is an example of an arbitrary meaning that becomes satisfying. One day I tried to make a sentence with no prepositions or articles—"Anybody can die, evidently." ABCDE. And once you've gone that far, you want to see—"Anybody can die, evidently. Few go happily." Then it becomes irresistible to finish the alphabet. Of course you know as an experienced abecedarian that around X it's going to get very tricky.

What makes that a poem?

If it is a poem, and thank you, what makes it a poem is the cadences. The bodily presence of the poem. I hope that as it goes through the alphabet, it has rhythms that qualify it as a poem. The test is to say it in your voice, to say it aloud to yourself or to imagine hearing it aloud.

ABC

Any body can die, evidently. Few
Go happily, irradiating joy,

Knowledge, love. Most
Need oblivion, painkillers,
Quickest respite.

Sweet time unafflicted,
Various world:
X = your zenith.

A-B-C-D-E . . . right through to Z! So it is true that when you were young you roamed the dictionary!

Yes, I spent many hours with a dictionary. I used to love the fact that it had no story. It didn't go anywhere. My mind could roam freely from word to word. I would set out to see if *reverse* and *converse* had anything in common, and on the way from *converse* to *reverse* I might come upon a word in the *D*'s like *dirndl*. I think I know what *dirndl* is—some kind of skirt—but I would wonder what language it came from, and whether there are other words in English that begin with *dr* and some other consonant. It was just—well, it was just fun.

My favorite period in English poetry is the sixteenth century. My favorite poets are people like Ben Jonson and Thomas Campion and Fulke Greville. I treasure that period for the sweetness and gracefulness of the English language—for example, Campion's poem "Now winter nights enlarge / The number of their hours; / And clouds their storms discharge / Upon the airy towers. / Let now the chimneys blaze / And cups o'erflow with wine, / Let well-tuned words amaze / With harmony divine. / Now yellow waxen lights / Shall wait on honey love / While youthful revels, masques, and courtly sights / Sleep's leaden spells remove."—it's rather like Mozart, delicious to hear. This is the period Keats drew on, and Hart Crane, and Allen Ginsberg. Thinking is a good thing. I'm in favor of intelligence and knowledge. But if you live too much in your head, without any bodily sense of poetry, I don't think you'll truly get poetry. It's very revealing to me to hear Garrison Keillor read a poem aloud on *Prairie Home Companion* or *Writer's Almanac*. You hear Garrison read a poem and you say, This man understands poetry. You don't have to hear him yak about it. You can hear the understanding in his voice.

Radio seems such an appropriate medium for poetry, but what about your work on the Internet? You're poetry editor of Slate, *the Microsoft publication.*

I choose the poems in *Slate*, and each week the poem is read aloud. If you have a sound card on your computer, you can click it on and hear the poet read the poem aloud. And if it's a dead poet—Thomas Hardy or Emily Dickinson—you hear me read it. There's a lot of poetry on the Web, there are hundreds of poetry sites. People post their work on the Web. There are modern poetry magazines and a lot of classic poetry. You can go to a Robert Burns site or a Keats site. Oddly enough, poetry may be a medium that fits the computer very well. People don't want to read a long, episodic novel off a monitor, but poetry fits. In these ways the medium goes back to the individual, to the bodily part of poetry, because you can hear it. And you can join a community at the same time. *Slate* has chat groups in a feature called "The Fray." I went on-line in real time recently, and the callers were typing their messages and I was answering their questions. Very likable people. I don't know what they look like, and most of them are using pseudonyms, but they're quite generous to one another, and we had a lively session.

Poetry seems so much a part of normal life to hear you talk about it, and yet we are told that for many people poetry is removed from ordinary life. Is there a way to close the gap?

I am not sure that *gap* is the right word. I think there is a kind of unrecognized quality to the love of poetry in this country, for reasons that are very American. Some countries are united by a single folk tradition. In some countries a social class gives a certain cache and coherence to the national culture—for people to show they're cultured they must be able to quote a few lines of the great national poet, even if it's sham. Here, we Americans are many different folk. There's no one unifying folk culture. My own post is a typical American invention in progress. We're making it up as we go along. I think you know we've been conducting the Favorite Poem project, asking Americans to send us the title and author of a poem they value, with a few sentences about the poem's personal importance for them. We want to create an archive on video and audio of what people do with their voices and faces when asked to say aloud a poem we love. The passion, diversity, and unpredictable drama of the responses we've seen assure me that it's a worthwhile project. We've received more than ten thousand letters and E-mail messages from all fifty states, the Virgin Islands and Puerto Rico, written by a striking variety of Americans—from ages six to ninety-seven, from New York to Los Angeles and from Anchorage, Alaska, to Bettendorf, Iowa. The occupations of volunteers include beekeepers, belly dancers, corporate executives, singers, painters, pipe fitters, trapeze artists. The database of letters, which is in itself a resource, gives a rich picture of the American people at the turn of the millennium. The poems they've chosen are varied, too. Frost is the most often chosen poet, and Walt Whitman, Emily Dickinson, William Shakespeare, and W. B. Yeats are also well represented. But there are also poems by Sappho, Catullus, Chidiock Tichborne, Li Po, Alexander Pope, Eavan Boland, and Yusef Komunyakaa (and of course popular favorites like Eugene Field, Robert Service, and "Casey at the Bat"). There are more than a dozen languages represented—Persian, German, Polish, Japanese, and Yiddish among them. We've heard from a good number of students, which is encouraging. My dearest wish is that the finished archive can be used in such a way that it affects teaching—that it makes a personal and indeed physical relationship to a poem an important part of the study of poetry. One way that may be accomplished is via the Internet. We've just launched the project website at www.favoritepoem.org. I hope the site will expand to include all of the audiovisual segments.

Let's hear one of your favorite poems—one of your own.

When I was first thinking about the history hidden in every moment, in our bodies and artifacts and words, I happened to be musing about the old treadle sewing machines: that beautiful wrought-iron work, the graceful contour of the arm with its gold ornaments against the black, the wood with its inset steel, the efficiency of the belt. I was thinking about the machines, not shirts in particular.

At some point I thought about how the word *treadle* chimed with *needle*. Then I had *bobbin* and *union*, and from there it took off, guided by the sounds but calling up a lot of lore I had been collecting all my life: Hobsbaum's essay about the industrial origin of the kilt, the traditional skills of the presser and cutter in the garment industry, the eighteenth-century hoax of Ossian, and so forth.

Shirt

The back, the yoke, the yardage. Lapped seams.
The nearly invisible stitches along the collar
Turned in a sweatshop by Koreans or Malaysians

Gossiping over tea and noodles on their break
Or talking money or politics while one fitted
This armpiece with its overseam to the band

Of cuff I button at my wrist. The presser, the cutter,
The wringer, the mangle. The needle, the union,
The treadle, the bobbin. The code. The infamous blaze

At the Triangle Factory in nineteen-eleven.
One hundred and forty six died in the flames
On the ninth floor, no hydrants, no fire escapes—

The witness in a building across the street
Who watched how a young man helped a girl to step
Up to the window sill, then held her out

Away from the masonry wall and let her drop.
And then another. As if he were helping them up
To enter a streetcar, and not eternity.

A third before he dropped her put her arms
Around his neck and kissed him. Then he held
Her into space, and dropped her. Almost at once

He stepped to the sill himself, his jacket flared
And fluttered up from his shirt as he came down,
Air filling up the legs of his gray trousers—

Like Hart Crane's Bedlamite, "shrill shirt ballooning."
Wonderful how the pattern matches perfectly
Across the placket and over the twin bar-tacked

Corners of both pockets, like a strict rhyme
Or a major chord. Prints, plaids, checks,
Houndstooth, Tattersall, Madras. The clan tartans

Invented by mill-owners inspired by the hoax of Ossian,
To control their savage Scottish workers, tamed
By a fabricated heraldry: MacGregor,

Bailey, MacMartin. The kilt, devised for workers
To wear among the dusty clattering looms.
Weavers, carders, spinners. The loader,

The docker, the navvy. The planter, the picker, the sorter
Sweating at her machine in a litter of cotton
As slaves in calico headrags sweated in fields:

George Herbert, your descendant is a Black
Lady in South Carolina, her name is Irma
And she inspected my shirt. Its color and fit

And feel and its clean smell have satisfied
Both her and me. We have culled its cost and quality
Down to the buttons of simulated bone,

The buttonholes, the sizing, the facing, the characters
Printed in black on neckband and tail. The shape,
The label, the labor, the color, the shade. The shirt.

There's a lot of life in that poem, a lot of life and history in an ordinary shirt.

The poem itself is an artifact fed by many ancient streams—I hope—just as any shirt is.

The Poets

Poet biographies adapted from the work of the Geraldine R. Dodge Poetry Festival staff.

COLEMAN BARKS

Barks earned his B.A. and Ph.D. degrees from the University of North Carolina at Chapel Hill and his M.A. from the University of California at Berkeley and went on to teach for thirty years at the University of Georgia in Athens, where he recently retired and was named Professor Emeritus of English. In 1976, Robert Bly showed Barks scholarly translations of the ecstatic poems of Jelaluddim Rumi, the thirteenth-century Sufi mystic who is said to be as famous in the Islamic world as Shakespeare is in the West. "These poems need to be released from their cages," Bly said, and Barks took up the challenge. In collaboration with the Persian linguist John Moyne, he has become the primary conduit for bringing Rumi's mystical consciousness to Americans, translating and publishing fifteen collections of Rumi's poems, including *The Illuminated Rumi* (1997) and his upcoming book, *The Glance*. Barks often collaborates in poetry readings with the Paul Winter Consort and with the dancer-storyteller Zuleikha.

LORNA DEE CERVANTES

Born in San Francisco's Mission District, Cervantes is of Native American and Mexican ancestry. She began writing poetry when she was eight and was published in Mexican and American newspapers and literary reviews by the time she was twenty. In 1974 she taught herself printing and founded her own literary journal and press—both called *Mango*—to publish Chicano and Chicana writers. Her first book, *Emplumada*, won the 1982 American Book Award, and her second book, *From the Cables of Genocide* (1991), won the Paterson Poetry Prize and the Latino Literature Prize. A recipient of grants from the National Endowment for the Arts and the Lila Wallace Reader's Digest Fund Writers Award, she is Associate Professor at the University of Colorado at Boulder.

MARK DOTY

Doty's six books of poetry include *Atlantis* (1995) and *The Sweet Machine* (1998). Among his many honors are the National Book Critics Circle Award for *My Alexandria* (1993) and the Witter Bynner Prize for Poetry. He has contributed poems to *A Place Apart: A Cape Cod Reader* (1993) and *The Name of Love: Classic Gay Male Love Poems* (1995). He recently published a memoir, *Heaven's Coast*. Doty, who has taught at

Goddard College, Sarah Lawrence College, and the University of Utah, presently teaches at the University of Houston. He is the recipient of fellowships from the Guggenheim Foundation and the National Endowment for the Arts.

DEBORAH GARRISON

Born in Ann Arbor, Michigan, in 1965, Garrison graduated from Brown University with a thesis in creative writing. She later joined the editorial staff of *The New Yorker*, where she is currently a senior nonfiction editor. Her poetry has appeared in the pages of *The New Yorker*, *Elle*, *The New York Times*, and *Slate* on-line. Her first collection, *A Working Girl Can't Win*, was published in 1998. Deborah Garrison lives with her husband and their infant daughter in Montclair, New Jersey.

JANE HIRSHFIELD

Hirshfield is the editor and co-translator of two anthologies, *Women in Praise of the Sacred: Forty-three Centuries of Spiritual Poetry by Women* (1994) and *The Ink Dark Moon: Love Poems by Ono no Komachi and Izumi Shikibu, Women of the Ancient Court of Japan* (1990). Born in New York City and educated at Princeton University, she has lived in Northern California for the past twenty years. She is the recipient of fellowships from the Guggenheim and Rockefeller Foundations and is currently on the faculty of the Bennington Writing Seminars. Her own poetry was recently published in *The Lives of the Heart*, and a collection of her essays entitled *Nine Gates: Entering the Mind of Poetry* was also published.

THE POETS

STANLEY KUNITZ

Kunitz welcomed his ninetieth year in 1995 with a new collection of poems, *Passing Through*. He has received nearly every honor bestowed upon a poet, including the Pulitzer and Bollingen Prizes, a National Medal of Arts from President Clinton in 1993, and the Shelley Memorial Award from the Poetry Society of America in 1995. He served as consultant in poetry to the Library of Congress (now called U.S. Poet Laureate), State Poet of New York, and Chancellor of the Academy of American Poets. As editor of the Yale Younger Poets Series from 1969 to 1977 and as a founder of both the Fine Arts Work Center in Provincetown, Massachusetts, and Poets House in New York City, he has promoted poetry and public access to the arts, encouraging many of the younger poets and artists who are now prominent figures in American culture. Kunitz and his wife, the painter Elise Asher, live in Provincetown and Greenwich Village in New York City.

KURTIS LAMKIN

Lamkin is currently touring the United States with a collection of poems entitled *El Shabazz* (CD, Jumbaco Sound). His poems have also been recorded on the CD *My Juju* (1995) and are included in *I Felt a Little Jumpy Around You* (1996). He has performed his poems and music internationally, from Sajara, Gambia (West Africa), to the Guggenheim Museum in New York. A native of Philadelphia, he taught in metropolitan New York public schools and community sites through Teachers & Writers Collaborative, and from 1994 to 1996 he was Poet in Residence at the New School for Social Research. He and his family live in Charleston, South Carolina.

SHIRLEY GEOK-LIN LIM

Born in the British colony of Malacca, Malaysia, Lim is now an American citizen. Arriving in Boston in 1969, she studied with J. V. Cunningham, to whom she dedicated her first book of poems, *Crossing the Peninsula* (1980). Winner of the Commonwealth Prize, Lim received a Ph.D. in English and American Literature from Brandeis University and is currently Professor of English and Chair of Women's Studies at the University of California at Santa Barbara. Author of four books of poetry, three collections of stories, and two critical books, she has twice received the American Book Award—for her memoir, *Among the White Moon Faces* (1996), and for the coedited anthology *The Forbidden Stitch: An Asian American Women's Anthology* (1989). Her most recent collection of poems is entitled *What the Fortune Teller Didn't Say*. She has also been a Fulbright Distinguished Lecturer.

PAUL MULDOON

Muldoon was born in Northern Ireland in 1951 and is currently Howard G. B. Clark Professor at Princeton University, where he chairs the creative writing program. *Hay* (1998) is his tenth volume of poetry; poems from the earlier books are gathered in *New Selected Poems, 1968–1994* (1996). He received his B.A. from Queen's University in Belfast, where he studied with Seamus Heaney, and he was a radio and television producer with the BBC in Northern Ireland for thirteen years until moving to the United States in the late 1980s. His work as an editor, translator, librettist, and poet has earned him a Guggenheim Fellowship, the T. S. Eliot Prize, and the *Irish Times* Award for Poetry.

MARGE PIERCY

Born into a working-class family in Detroit, Michigan, Piercy became the first in her family to attend college. She won scholarships for her writing and published her first novel, *Going Down Fast*, in 1969. She has written thirteen books of poetry and fourteen books of prose, winning—among many awards—the venerable Golden Rose for poetry and an Arthur C. Clarke Award for science fiction. She is the poetry editor of *Tikkun* magazine and lives with her husband, the writer Ira Wood, on Cape Cod.

ROBERT PINSKY

Pinsky was recently named to an unprecedented third term as Poet Laureate of the United States. The son of an optician and grandson of a local tavern owner, he grew up along the pleasure-pier scenery of Long Branch, New Jersey, a once thriving seaside resort. He has published four volumes of original poems, recently collected in *The Figured Wheel: New and Collected Poems, 1966–1996.* His translation of Dante's *Inferno*, which renders the poem in the cadences of spoken English, became a bestseller. In addition to teaching in the Graduate Writing Program and English Department at Boston University, Pinsky is poetry editor of the on-line magazine *Slate*. The recipient of many awards for his poems, translations, and prose works, he most recently was awarded the Lenore Marshall Poetry Prize by *The Nation* and the Academy of American Poets. His latest books are an anthology of poems, *Handbook of Heartbreak*, and *The Sounds of Poetry: A Brief Guide*.

PERMISSIONS

Permission to use the poems reprinted in this book was granted by the following: